From Piety to Politics

From Piety to Politics
The Evolution of
Sufi Brotherhoods

Barbara DeGorge

 New Academia Publishing, LLC
Washington, DC

Copyright © 2005 by Barbara DeGorge

New Academia Publishing, 2006

All rights reserved. No part of this book may be reproduced or transmitted in any form or by any means, electronic or mechanical, including photocopying, recording, or by any information storage and retrieval system.

Printed in the United States of America

Library of Congress Control Number: 2005931974
ISBN 0-9744934-9-X paperback (alk. paper)

New Academia Publishing, LLC
P.O. Box 27420, Washington, DC 20038-7420
www.newacademia.com - info@newacademia.com

Contents

Preface and Acknowledgments   vii

Introduction	1
1. Modernization Theory Questioned	9
2. A Brief History of Sufism	21
3. A History of Sudanese Sufi Orders through the Khatmiyya	31
Early Tariqa Phase	
Eighteen Century Taruq	
The Khatmiyya	
4. The Mahdiyya	51
5. Political Evolution	65
Authority	
The Body Politique	
The Mahdist Government	
Modern Political Involvement	
6. Sufi Millenarianism in China	91
Conclusion	111
Notes	119
Glossary	141
Bibliography	144
Index	152

Preface and Acknowledgments

The following study traces the evolution of Sufi brotherhoods in both the Sudan and China in order to show how they evolved to become political forces. It displays how the Islamic world holds vehicles and methods to elicit a response from Muslim communities in face of modernization and foreign influence. It is a work that is not meant to assert that Islam is a modern religion enabling liberal democratization. Rather, this work seeks to illustrate that Islam is able to accommodate change by use of its own internal structure.

During the course of this research, I have become indebted to many people who have offered their help and their suggestions most generously. Although it is impossible to name everyone who offered their support, it is necessary to mention those without whose help this study would never have been possible.

First and foremost, I would like to give my deepest thanks and gratitude to Dr. John Voll of the Muslim-Christian Center for Understanding: History and International Affairs at the Edmund A. Walsh School of Foreign Service, Georgetown University, Washington DC, who is the undisputed expert in Sudanese Sufism. His valuable suggestions and critical comments have greatly facilitated the research for this study. Not only has his expertise been invaluable, but I will always treasure his friendship and be appreciative for his emotional support throughout this process.

My thanks are owed also to Dr. Gabriel Warburg, who is an expert on the Sudan and has written more than ten books on the subject, for his immeasurable support and especially for his encouragement. I also thank the late Dr. Nehemiah Levtzion for taking time from his busy schedule for meeting and discussing this project with me. Thank you to Dr. Yehudit Ronen, Tel Aviv University, who started out as an advisor and has become an invaluable friend.

All projects like this have people behind the scenes who unknowingly contribute to its success. Thank you to Mehvesh Farooqi, my assistant for taking the time to read and correct errors in the manuscript. Thank you to my colleagues who encouraged me to finish the book, and thank you to Lance de Masi. Without knowing it, you have provoked me to think and evaluate many things, which led to the completion of the project, as well as undertaking new ones.

Last but not least, I would like to extend my deepest appreciation and love to my husband Charles and my children, Ari, Thal, and Charlie for their patience while I completed this work. My husband's quiet support of what I love to do has enabled me to be the best I can and pursue my dreams. Thank you all for your love, support and patience.

Introduction

Islam is an enigma to the Western world. It has no political ideologies, especially those that coincide with the twenty-first century. It is backward, violent and completely undemocratic. Islam reacts to events and its reactions are customarily anti-western and anti-modern. This is one of the most disturbing perceptions today of how the West views Islam — both as a religion and a culture, especially in the political arena. As there are only a handful of Muslim countries that have embraced some sort of democracy or democratic traditions, the most obvious assumption is that Islamic countries cannot and will not be able to ever become democratic in any sense of the word that those from the West understand. This is because the Western world is educated to think of a political system in terms of a liberal democracy. It is usually very difficult to accept political systems outside of the scope of democracy that are considered normal and acceptable to other people. Because of this Western education, Islam is basically perceived of as a religion that impedes any type of development or modernity. This assumption is even more prevalent in the events since September 2001.

However, this premise is actually quite false. It is first necessary to accept that most of what impedes the democratization and modernization of Islam is based more the tradition of the people than what is contained in its religious doctrines. Moreover, unlike Western countries that developed their democratic ideals through contact with each other, Muslim society did not have any neighboring country from which to draw that experience. The contact Islam has had in its growth and development been one that incorporated others into their way of life. However, that is not to say that Islam has no contact with concepts of democracy. Actually, Islam holds certain modernizing elements that go back to its inception, especially within the political sphere.

Islam is much more than a simple religion. It is an all-encompassing way of life, which addresses all modalities: social, economical and political. The political tone within Islam was one that arose in the formation of the religion. As long as Muhammed was alive, he was the undisputed head of both the faith and the community. He subjugated all areas within his reach and pronounced himself the sovereign ruler. Laws were made, justice dispensed, taxes levied, war waged and peace concluded. In essence, Muhammed created a quasi government. However, the political overtones he set manifested themselves immediately following his death.

The first issue to confront the Islamic community was how to organize government after the death of Muhammed. Because this was a very central issue among Muslims, different vehicles for expressing political activism arose in the Islamic community. One such response came from Sufi brotherhoods (*tariqa, sing. taruq, pl.*). Sufi brotherhoods originally were established to be a guide to achieve a closer union with God. As time passed, they evolved from their initial essence to one that incorporated political activism and sectarianism. It is because of their politically active nature, Sufi brotherhoods have been able to speak for their communities and in many cases have transformed into viable political parties. It is their religious alliances that give them the ability to form a cohesive unit that has political power.

Since its inception, Islam has had a history of sectarianism (*taifiya*). Sectarianism in this sense refers to the religious alliances formed in the Islamic world, especially during periods of conflict. It demonstrates a continuing belief and loyalty of the religious orders. The Islamic community arose out of the prophetic revelations sent to Muhammed, but the spread of its message was accomplished basically through military conquests, *jihad*. Through the centuries, Islam has looked at itself, finding the need to revitalize and reform in order to keep the original message in tact. This expression is more commonly known as millennial Islam. It is one of "the means of expressing dissatisfaction with the state of society... when the Islamic community has felt imminent danger to its world of value and meaning."[1] This usually occurred with militant overtones, whether in strictly Muslim countries or in ones with a sizable Muslim population.

As Islam has been build upon tradition, it also has a history of *taqlid*, or the unquestioning imitation or following of tradition, past legal or doctrinal precedents. Although in its past, Islam has adapted and transformed, it was not until the nineteenth century that serious modern challenges emerged. Intense pressure was put on Islam to reexamine itself, its social structures and institutions. This was done as the majority of the Islamic world had come in contact with Western hegemony and its values. There was also the confrontation with those who considered themselves experts and critics of the authenticity of traditional Islamic Qur'anic literature. The perceived strength of the West forced questions of Islamic communities and required that action be taken to renew the glory and intrinsic power once found there.

There are many different regions where revival and reform occurred beginning at the middle of the nineteenth century. It was not particular to one or two regions. Many Islamic communities found that the casual expression of their identity was not sufficient to bind their communities together. In many of these instances, Sufi brotherhoods were the ones to initiate many movements of revitalization.

Sufi brotherhoods represent the mystical path within Islam. They are historically concerned with achieving an inner spirituality, and as such, are seemingly apolitical and outside of any secular activities. However, the nineteenth century was to change this perception, especially in region where there were sizable Sufi populations. Sufi brotherhoods illustrate that mystical religious orders have been able to transform into vehicles of political modernization and expression, even becoming modern political parties and interest groups. This has been noted many times by those who study Sufism, but the reasons why such a transformation has occurred has been rarely examined. Moreover, this phenomenon has occurred, especially during the nineteenth century in various places where there is both a majority and non-majority Islamic population. By examining this shift to political activism in Sufi brotherhoods, it is possible to identify the underlying causes in order to gain an understanding of the dynamics of certain Islamic groups and why they have been able to become a modern political force, expressing the goals of their followers.

An examination of this type is important inasmuch as Western stereotypes of Islam, especially with the resurgence of Islamic activism, are basically inaccurate. There is a fundamental misunderstanding between the West and Islamic world in regards to political thought and action. The West is unable to comprehend that Islam is able to transform from within to meet the constant changes occurring in the modern world, particularly in the political and economic arena. It is inconceivable that Islam, especially Sufism, has the innate ability to adapt itself. Sufi brotherhoods, however, are excellent examples of how Islam is able to change from traditional religious affiliations into modern secular ones, exercising power in the political arena.

In order to gain a basic understanding of the evolution of the Sufi brotherhoods, two Sufist movements will be studied. By examining and contrasting movements in two diverse regions, it is easier to put the entire phenomenon into a global explanation. In each instance, one can see that if taken as a separate incidence, the comprehensive significance of the activism occurring is not readily seen or understood. But when incidences occur concurrently, and are examined within that context, the significance of the actions taking place contains more noteworthy implications. Thus, the purpose of this study is to explain why brotherhoods transformed into modern political parties and as well as becoming a vehicle to express dissatisfaction with a governing power, seen which will be in the case studies of the Sudan[2] and China respectively.

The following chapter looks at the methods and ideologies that have arisen through political modernization theory to see if the political power achieved could possibly fit into these paradigms. Although the modernization theories of the 1960s have been previously considered passé, there has been a trend to revisit them. Not all components of these theories are useful; however, they do provide a framework in which one is able to analyze particularities occurring within a political setting, especially from a western perspective. By applying the components in modernization theories, one is able to gain a better understanding of the transformations occurring.

In order to understand its legitimacy as a political force, Sufism must be briefly examined to show how it originally acquired legitimacy within the Islamic world. A careful investigation of the historical rise of the brotherhoods to political activism will be made by analyzing two movements in two different regions in the world: the Sudan and China. In the Sudan, the Khatmiyya and Mahdiyya in particular offer a look into the evolution of classical Sufism to political activism. An analysis of their internal structure and the authority held by their leaders indicates that modern paradigms are expressionless since Islam has been its own modernizing force since its conception. Furthermore, evidence suggests that Sufism and its internal setup are similar to those advocated by Western paradigms of modernization.

This investigation contributes further not only as to why the Khatmiyya and Mahdiyya became legitimate political forces within an Islamic context, but a modern one as well. The study underlines the fact that the millennial experience in the Sudan was not an isolated case at the time when it began. Because lines of communication went past the borders of countries, millennial Sufism appeared in many places at the same time. To show how the lines of communication and brotherhood cohesiveness influenced similar expressions of dissatisfaction, the nineteenth century revival and reform movement started by the Sufi brotherhood, the Naqsbandiyya, in China is explored. The correlation of events in these two regions will demonstrate that Sufi brotherhoods by nature of their intrinsic internal and external organization are not only political forces, but modernizing ones as well.

Islam first made inroads into the Sudan before the eleventh century by the Arab Muslims involved with the caravan trade from Cairo, and then was spread by tribal leaders. Most of the penetration into sub-Sahara Africa is attributed, today, to the Almorvids (*al-Murābitūn*) who were the chief promulgators of the religion in the eleventh century.[3] However, the Arabization of the Sudan came from the penetration of Arab tribes (*qabila, sing. qaba'ilun pl.*),[4] which were already established in the upper Nile valley region.[5] By the middle of the fifteenth century, these Arab nomadic tribes were responsible for the Islamization and Arabization of the three Christian kingdoms in the present-day country of Sudan.[6] With the beginning of the Funj sultanate in 1504,[7] Sudanese Islam entered into a three hundred year period of expansion. One of the principal elements for the growth of Islam in the Sudanese area was Sufism, which was being carried throughout the Islamic empire during this period by nomadic merchants, teachers, and Muslim soldiers. As it will be shown, the Sufi groups that developed would be quite successful in spreading Islam. In addition, through an examination of the two major brotherhoods, the Khatmiyya and the Mahdiyya, it will be demonstrated how the loosely organized Sudanese Sufi brotherhoods were able to manifest themselves into a major political force. This evolution has permitted Sufi orders to become two of the main political parties in the Sudan.

The Sudan, however, is not the only place where Sufism acted as a political force, or one that bound the Islamic community together. As will be further shown, Sufism acted as an impetus in China at approximately the same time as it did in the Sudan, pulling together a disjointed Islamic population. It gave Chinese Muslims the opportunity to express both their identity and cohesiveness in light of having an appreciable population in a non-Muslim country. The Chinese Islamic experience demonstrates that although rebellion has traditionally been a part of Chinese history, the movement that occurred in the Muslim community was not case specific to China, nor had its roots only in the discord that was occurring then. As in the Sudan, the Chinese movement proved that Sufi brotherhoods were a political force, expressing the desires of its followers and responding to the changes occurring with modernity.

1

Modernization Theory Questioned

> It seems obvious, for example, that in the Islamic world and elsewhere, religious beliefs and institutions cannot simply be relegated to the ash cans of history under the "inevitable" onslaught of "secularism", nor can the former be dismissed as part of traditional society to be superseded.[8]

One of the greatest myths when one speaks of modernization is that religion cannot be a force that provokes or enables it. Religion is a hindrance to the idea that there is progress and innovation. Religion stagnates ideas, especially in the political arena. Yet, many people in the world hold deeply religious beliefs, reacting to political issues from the perspective of their religious heritage and traditions, especially in the Muslim world. The majority of those who advocate modernization reject the idea of traditional people and their societies being able to modernize under the impetus of their own. Because of this attitude, political scientists and historians do not know how to classify Islam as it presents itself as a traditional, yet modernizing force. By virtue of its seemingly rigid nature, Islam is perceived as an obstacle, instead of an impetus, in conveying the Muslim world into the new millennium and keeping pace with its Western counterparts, particularly with the appearance in the past years of fundamentalist movements. What must be considered is if Islam is really so unyielding in its basic system of belief so that modernization becomes out of the question and therefore is unable to keep up with the rapidly changing times.

Recent years have seen a resurgence of Islam under the term of *Islamic fundamentalism*.[9] The use of this term, however, is a misnomer. Fundamentalism is an affirmation of a particular faith, defined in a pure and literal manner. Originally it applied to a Christian experience that manifested itself during the early twentieth century as a response to what was thought at the time to be modernism. It is a belief in the inerrancy of the scripture, which cannot apply to Muslims, especially as all Muslims whether fundamentalist or not believe in the literal accuracy of their scripture. Islamic Fundamentalism can not be categorized as such an experience; it is an ideological phenomenon, not a single doctrine or movement. The term Islamic fundamentalism actually comes from western journalists who do not know any other way to characterize the phenomenon occurring around them. Muslims themselves formally use the term *tajdid*, which means "renewal." Within this context, it is a call to revive and revitalize or renew the Islamic religion to its glorious past, both religiously and politically. Islam has a long history in the belief of revival and reform, encompassing ideas of political and social activism that dates from the early Islamic times until the present. Therefore, according to many Islamic scholars, the term Islamic "radicalism," "revivalism" or "activism" more appropriately represents the current movement better. These terms reflect a reaction against what is considered westernization and takes a rejectionist stance, instead of one of adaptation. This is not to say that modernization is being discarded. What is being rejected is the notion that the only way to modernize and enter the new millennium is throw out old ideas and traditions in favor for what we in the West judge to politically correct and acceptable. Islam in essence has entered into its own activism to contend with the modern world and the problems arising with modernity.

In many ways, Western countries see this revival of Islam as a threat to both Western ideology and modernization. The Westerner is unable to understand or cope with any political ideology or activity that is seen as outside the scope of its own theories. What has been good for the West must therefore logically follow to be good for the rest of the world. In order to bring what has been conceived as a third world or undeveloped country into the sphere of Western thought, modernization and development theories were developed in the mid twentieth century. These theories were thought to be able to bring traditional communities into the modern world. One of the regions, these theorists or modernizationist hoped to modernize or westernize was the Islamic countries as it was perceived that traditional Islam will throw the Muslim countries back to the Dark Ages. Although the Dark Ages refers to a past European experience, Western perceptions in this respect are being transferred to Islam. Actually, during the European Dark Ages, Islam was at the height of its civilization. Because the modernization and development theories beginning in the 1960s developed mainly in the West, this fallacy has been attributed to Islam.

It is necessary to digress at this point to discuss exactly what is meant by tradition. The word tradition is a term of which the connotations can be varied and in many cases even contradictory. The term used here implies the practice of Islam as it is put down in the Qur'an, the *Sunna* and the *Hadiths* in their purest forms.. It could be said to be the practices that are pre-modern. However, as it can be argued that Islam does not have a modern and pre-modern stage, the implication and the meaning that is used here of the word "tradition" are those practices that have not changed since the beginning of Islam.

But what is actually meant by modernization theory? Modernization implies the introduction of political and economical organizations, along with the techniques of production, communication and transportation that are characteristic of Western societies. In essence, it is a modification of the structures of indigenous non-Western society, which Westerners characterize as "traditional." It is 'traditional' because the West perceives non-Western indigenous groups as being a part of a primitive past. Thus, to the West, traditional is considered as a form of uncivilized and ignorant behavior patterns, especially in economics and politics. In this sense, tradition is being defined as the "set of practices, normally governed by overtly or tacitly accepted rules and of a ritual or symbolic nature, which seek to inculcate certain values and norms of behavior of repetition, which automatically implies continuity with the past."[10] As a result, the Westerner is ascribing his set of rules and behavior patterns to non-Western societies, designating them as being part of the Western past, which no longer can exist in the face of modernization.

Accordingly, modernization theory is studied from the perspective of economic development, the process of industrialization; the psychological and social changes in society; and political transformations, the structures, national awareness, and participation of the masses. Modernization is primarily characterized by a move away from traditional irrational, emotional behavior to one grounded in rational and scientific control. It is a revolt against tradition, as described above, and historically classical authority of all kinds, especially a religiously oriented one. Man is at the center, putting human interests above everything and promising unlimited potentialities. Modernization is, in this sense, a move towards a modern society has been characterized by what could be termed a:

> "world culture"—based on advanced technology and the spirit of science, on a rational view of life, a secular approach to social relations, a feeling for

justice in public affairs, and, above all else, on the acceptance in the political realm of the belief that the prime unit of the polity should be the nation-state.[11]

It is a process in which non-Western countries take on the characteristics of the West. The West is categorized as the more developed societies. The emphasis is on a rapid and total change or transformation of what is considered the less developed, to a stereotype of the more developed society.[12] Modernization, therefore, means to embrace westernization and secularization. Secularization, especially, is a *sine qua non* for modernization.

The modernization theories, which arose during the 1960s, were intended to not only bringing modern economic practices to the Third World but to encourage democracy as well. The majority of them argued political development, economic growth and social modernization were inclusive: one could not exist without the other. It is important to distinguish that these theories all encompassed industrialization. They all hold what may be termed as a universalistic approach; that is "modernization means fundamentally a process which is an inevitable concomitant of industrialization, or more accurately, 'modern economic growth.' "[13] There can only be a complete change in the societal, political, and economic structure if industrialization takes place. This would allow the underdeveloped, or Third World, country to enter into the world economy. Immanual Wallerstein defines it as a world system that lacks political centralization and unification. It is therefore, not only a multiplicity of cultures, but a majority of sovereign political units.[14] This means that one has to embrace capitalism as it is the only system that could exist today. James Coleman's theory of modernization is a prime example of this type of thought process. All the six points put forth by him encompass westernization, secularization, economic growth and the introduction of western political interest parties.[15]

The high point of this type of developmentalist theory was epitomized in *The Politics of Developing Areas* written also by Coleman and co-authored by Gabriel Almond. They asserted that all countries are able to follow a "functionalist plan" that was universally applicable.[16] This particular theory, unfortunately, had severe problems since it was strikingly similar to the functions found in the American democratic process. Although Almond argued that the theory applied universally, when analyzed, this tripartite system of government was nothing more than an abstraction to developing Third World countries, especially those, organized around traditional governmental structures, i.e. Kings, councils, and the like.

Probably the most striking characteristic of modernization, disengagement, was asserted by Samuel Huntington. Disengagement means, according to Huntington, a shift away from any traditional point of authority. Religious, familial, traditional, and ethnic authorities are replaced by a single, secular national political authority.[17] In order for a nation to enter into the modern world, there must be a disengagement from traditional values, language, rhetoric and, most importantly, from traditional authority. What Huntington essentially was asserting a move away from indigenous customs and value systems, and customary forms of authority that were not in the Western modality. Thus, disengagement means moving from communal loyalty to a national loyalty. According to French sociologist Gustave Lebon: "To respect tradition is a condition of existence for a people; to know how to disengage from it, a condition of progress."[18] Especially in a religious community such as Islam, this means that there must be a redefinition of the religious community in relation to the state. The emotional identification of the religious community—Islam—must be supplemented by political loyalty, thus making Islam secondary to the state.[19] In essence, tradition and political loyalty must be differentiated, as they are incompatible with each other.

Most Westerners and Muslims educated in Western countries seem to hold this viewpoint. The Western-based process of modernization is considered as a necessity. The basic perception is that if Islamic countries do not embrace modernization in the form of westernization and secularization, how are they ever going to be able to enter the modern world as viable nation-states? According to the occidental standpoint, tradition - certainly one that is religiously oriented - is completely opposed to modernization. Consequently, Islam cannot be a vehicle for modernization. According to Western thought, the traditional values of Islam are most likely to hinder the social transformations that are necessary in modernization. Westerners overlook that what is classified, as tradition in religion is not an invented tradition. It is a time honored practice and belief, handed down from generation to generation, which is adaptable to changing conditions and times without losing its intrinsic idea. That is not to say that this type of tradition cannot be classified as an "invented tradition" at some point in history. All tradition evolves from some human desire to ritualize themselves.[20] However, within the confines of a religious definition, tradition has withstood the test of time, thus proving its continuity. According to Terence Ranger and Eric Hobsbawn: "where old ways are alive, traditions need neither be revived nor invented."[21] Therefore, tradition does not necessitate transformation to be responsive to outside changes, especially those rapidly occurring since the Industrial revolution.

The indigenous elite in non-western countries historically have adapted and tried to duplicate the ideals of modernization formulated by early imperialism in their countries, changing 'traditional' institutions. Governmental structures and economic practices had been patterned on Western paradigms. However, while the few select westernized elite have adopted this stance, the majority of the Islamic population holds a religious orientation both in their minds and culture. Muslims hold beliefs, stemming from the Qur'an, of how their society should function with specific practices. They are not prepared or able to give up these customary beliefs and behaviors containing their own internal language as modernization require them to do. It is a way of life for them, which they feel adequately meets any outside challenge. This is known in Islamic terminology as *taqlid*. Therefore, modernization does not entail the westernization and secularization of their mode of living and communication. As noted by Daniel Crecelius in his article "The Course of Secularization in Modern Egypt" and John L. Esposito in *The Islamic Threat:*

> Most studies on the process of modernization or secularism recognize the necessity for all systems by which man lives, the psychological and intellectual, no less than the political and economic, to undergo transformation. We do not find this change in Egypt, whether at the level of the state or society, except among a small minority of Westernized individuals. Traditional beliefs, practices and values reign supreme among Egypt's teeming village population and among the majority of the urban masses. It should be emphasized that adherence to tradition is not confined to any single class or group of occupations, but is characteristic of a broad spectrum of all Egyptian classes.[22]

It is important to note that this does not negate modernization taking place. Modernization does occur, but not by transference. The above case used by Crecelius and Esposito illustrates the gradual transformation to modernization, taking place over centuries without displacing society. In this respect, the process of modernization does not ignore historical evolution. Rather, it makes room for diverse societal developments, therefore giving different societies the room to develop within their own cultural framework. What is important to realize is that, as pointed out by the John and Jean Comaroff, modernity does not follow only one path. There are many different types of modernities and modernizing influences.[23] Not even proponents of Western modernization paradigms have been able to agree on a specific method to bring about complete change and transformation.

As a result, tradition becomes a way to achieve modernity. Rationalization and disengagement had been considered the only way to modernize. This has now changed to include an acceptance of a diversity of modernizing expressions. In place of rationalization and disengagement, there are distinct types of modernizing responses, from the return of indigenous practices such as witchcraft to adherence to formalized ritual.[24] Ritual particularly has enabled societies to deal with the complex realities in the political arena. Since ritual has always been present in all cultures and societies, it is "...a vital element in the processes that make and remake social facts and collective identities."[25] Ritual and the act of following rites can bind a community together and answer the demands of a modernizing society as the rite speaks the language that is accepted and known by all. This language manifests in symbols understood by the adherents of the rite, enabling modernizing processes to take place while not stripping a community of their inherent identity.

In economics and especially politics, the interests of the/a group are not only material or power oriented. Max Weber pointed out that the values denied by society actually play an important role in expressing the identities and goals of a particular group.

> As a separate structure, a political community can be said to exist only if, and in so far as, a community constitutes more than an 'economic group'; or, in other words, in so far as it possesses value systems

ordering matters other than the directly economic disposition of goods and services.[26]

In all societies, these values are exhibited in the form of symbols. With symbols, the values of a particular cultural group become apparent, and then they are manifested through a symbolic language. This symbolic language is an extremely crucial factor in politics as it becomes a remarkably powerful tool of persuasion. Persuasion in all societies is basically an act of communication, and the methods utilized to communicate are then transformed into a type of political expressiveness. The language does not necessarily have to be in the form of speech, but can be a symbolic language, such as found in the Islamic religion.

In the Islamic religion, there is not only political language but also the language of politics. In the Muslim communities, there are myriad ways to communicate with each other. The Islamic language is in actuality more than just speech. It encompasses a way of life, and the understood language is one that is rich in symbolic meaning. These symbols are such that they can be manipulated for specific reasons. The language reaches not only the educated people, but influences the illiterate masses as well.

Therefore, as the Muslim elite become educated in their own respective countries, rising in political status, they have turned to religious language to communicate to their own population. This has consequently created states based on Islamic nationalism.[27] Religion therefore acts as a 'sacred language' binding the people together in an 'imagined community." Islam has been one such religion that not only has the ability to bind the people together with its sacred language, but the fact that Arabic is considered the sacred language of the Islamic text gives it an added force. Within Islam, political communication has evolved through the use of the traditional religious language comprehended by everyone. This has enabled modernization to take place as it invokes religious values and beliefs especially in the political arena. This type of communication has manifested itself in different forms throughout the Islamic world, ranging from utilizing Islam's historical roots in the Saudi peninsula to organized Sufi brotherhoods, from peaceful transformation to violent expressions.

The 1990s has seen a change in the attitude of Western modernists. For example, Samuel Huntington who advocated a disengagement from religious and indigenous practices, had done an about face. He now accepts that local beliefs and practices cannot be ignored.[28] Instead of a universal acceptance of the West and liberal democratic ideas, Huntington states that there has been an indigenization in non-Western countries since the beginning of the 1980s. According to his postulation, "the aim was no longer to modernize Islam, but to 'Islamize modernity'."[29] In a global sense, this means all non-Western countries are turning to their own indigenous practices and value systems in order to enter into and facilitate the modernizing process. The internal symbolic language understood by their constituency is appealed to, instead of the wholesale adoption of Westernization and secularization.

Huntington is not the only scholar to make this assessment. David Apter, another modernization proponent, has also made an about face in regards to non-Western indigenous societies. He now asserts that evolution and growth is a process that leads to democracy. Furthermore, in evaluating the course of change, one must take a tentative approach instead of reaching conclusions. According to Apter, it is too early for any concrete conclusions to be reached as the whole modernization process is undergoing dramatic changes.[30] Apter, along with Huntington, has realized that non-Western countries hold their own values and practices enabling them to respond and modernize under their own impetus.

In Islam, Sufi brotherhoods hold time-honored practices and beliefs that enable modernization to occur. This is because the ability to change or modernize is an inherent part of the Islamic religion. One of the major reasons that Islam has the ability to change is the concept of *ijtihad*, which signifies the independent analysis or interpretation of Islamic law. This idea is completely opposed to the concept of *taqlid*. While there are many Muslims who advocate *taqlid*, there are just as many who believe that there should be a process of change and adaptation within an Islamic context. Sufi Brotherhoods (*taruq, pl. tariqa, sing.*) have been an association within Islam that has proven to be a changing and modernizing force. They especially have been a strong force, uniting Muslims not only in Islamic regions, but also in areas where they are a minority. Two diverse examples one can point to are Sudan and China.

In Sudan and China, Sufi leaders were able to pull the masses together. Sufism has been an effective method of communication, acting as a force to pull a disjointed Muslim community together. In Sudan, the first sign of this was the strong organization of the *tariqa*, the Khatmiyya. This was then followed by the Mahdist revolution led by Muhammed Ahmad. The Mahdist Revolution was an impetus that consolidated the various tribal coalitions, transforming them into a nationalistic movement, allowing the Sudan to become an independent country. Sufism also was a force that permitted solely religious organizations to change into political parties. In China, it brought the Islamic community out of dormancy and enabled it to express itself within the violent political atmosphere of the time. Sufism, in its organizational hierarchy, not only satisfies the religious need in the masses of people, but acts as a "glue" to bind communities together to be the impetus in pushing into the modern world. Sufism speaks a language that incorporates religious standards, thus establishing methods to compel a society to transform itself.

2
A Brief History of Sufism

Sufism and Sufi Brotherhoods have historically proven to be able to elicit a modernizing response from its followers. However, this has not always been the case. Sufism has evolved and transformed over time, thus becoming an agent for modern political expression. However, to completely understand why Sufism became a vehicle for political activism, it is imperative to understand the history and development of Sufism and Sufi brotherhoods.

The Islamic religion began as a unified forced under the auspices of the Prophet Muhammed. When he died, the unity ended with Islam splitting into two separate factions. One group believed that Muhammed had designated his closest confidant and friend Abu Bakr to succeed him in leading the Muslim world and the other believed that he chose his son-in-law Ali to be his successor. These two factions have been known as Sunni and Shi'ite Muslims, respectively. The major difference between the Sunni and the Shi'ite Muslims is their doctrines of succession. The Shii doctrine is one that holds to the imamate, which says the leader of the Muslim people must be direct a descendant of the Prophet, versus the Sunni doctrine that states the leader should be chosen or elected as with the first Caliph.

This was not the only split that occurred within the Islamic religion. In the eighth century, there was a further split between the Shi'ite over the designated heir of the sixth imam,

Jafar al-Sadiq. This division resulted in the Ismailis (the Ismailis are also referred to as Seveners) and the Twelvers.[31] The political and religious unity of the Muslim community had begun to alter and as time passed, there were further divisions occurring. Some of these breaks occurred because there was dissent over basic doctrine, and others occurred as reactionary dissatisfaction to existing rule. Two such movements or growth of institutions that arose from the discontent with the Umayyad Caliphate were the ulema and the Sufis. The ulema were and are what is referred to as Islamic religious scholars and the Sufis are those who embrace mysticism.

Sufism

Separation and withdrawal from mainstream beliefs are apparent in all religions. Natural asceticism and the tendency to withdraw from the religious community have also been apparent in Islam. Those who separate themselves and follow a devotion of their own within the Islamic community are called Sufis. As Islam's foundation is the revealed word of the Prophet Muhammed (the Qur'an), Sufis are those who follow the prescribed practice of reading and studying the Qur'an. Because of this practice, Sufism became associated with certain practices and adherence, such as the dhikr. (The dhikr is usually a drawn out repetition of the word, Allah, the Muslim term for God. It also means a basic recitation, which is taught to those who follow Sufism.) The term Sufism in this work will signify any tendency in the Islamic religion holding there can be a direct communication between man and God.

In a broad sense, Sufism is the personalized, spiritual interiorization and intensification of the Islamic faith and its practices. Liberally defined, people who practice Sufism view themselves as Muslims who take Allah's call to perceive him both in the world as a whole, and within one's self. The Sufi is one who strives to have a close experience with Allah, ultimately leading to their absorption in him. It is a belief that they can have a direct experience with Allah by placing themselves in a state conducive to receive him. Additionally, it characterizes those who adhere to a way of life, incorporating certain rituals and tenets passed on by early Sufi teachers to obtain the desired state. Many non-Muslims look at this practice as Islamic mysticism or spiritualism, but that limits the actual meaning and belief.[32] It is, nevertheless, a mystical practice, running concomitantly with mainstream Islam, and usually has a connection with a divinatory revelation that is based in the Qur'an and *sharia* (Islamic law).

The word, Sufi, originates from "one who wears wool"(*Suf*). It comes from the Arabic word *tasawwuf*, connoting mysticism.[33] By the eighth century, it applied to those early Muslim ascetics who would don harsh woolen garments similar to those worn by a Christian monk. Over the next century, the term evolved to mean a group who separated themselves from others by giving emphasis on specific practices of the Qur'an and the *Sunna* (*Sunna* means the way or tradition of the Prophet, Mohammed). This did not mean they did not believe in Islamic law. Sufis accepted the legitimacy of it, but went beyond it. They adhered to a more rigid interpretation in order to establish the closer relationship with Allah. To the Sufi, it was not really necessary to have an established law, although in reality one can not see much of a difference between a Sufi and an orthodox Muslim. The basic difference is in the fact the Sufi puts more exceptional consequences to certain beliefs such as an absolute trust in God (*tawakkul*).[34] By the beginning of the ninth century, Sufism or "being a Sufi" came to mean those who were of the described group.[35]

Sufism emerged as a response to what was considered a laxity in following the traditions of the Prophet (*Sunna*). The first one hundred years of Islam were marked by a period of materialism and ostentatiousness, especially by those who were in high places as shown with the ornate architecture and art that was developed during the Umayyad period.[36] This ostentatiousness and display of wealth were seen by those in power as a way to legitimize their position and beliefs. As a natural reaction to this display, there was a tendency among some to turn inwards and away from worldly life. The emergence of Sufi Islam was, according to A. J. Arberry, a "reaction to the wealth and luxury that flooded the Islamic world after the conquest of Byzantium and the Persian Empire destroyed the simpler ways of life."[37] The early Sufi movement has best been described by Hasan al-Basri (643-728):

> He who is content, needing nothing, and who has sought peace; he who has trodden his carnal desires underfoot, will find freedom; he who had rid himself of envy will find friendship, and he who has patience for a little while will find himself prepared for eternity.[38]

Another great Islamic mystic, Husayn al Hallaj (858-922) portrayed this mysticism at its highest. According to al-Hallaj, each person shares in the Divine Will through an ecstatic joining with God where an exchange of individuality takes place between God and man: "I saw my Lord with my heart's eye and said, 'who are you? He answered, 'You.'"[39] One sees this same phenomenon happening in the beginning of Christianity once martyrdom was no longer necessary. Once Christianity was established as a legitimate religion, there were those who shunned the world and became monks and traveling priests in order to spread God's word. They too would dress in harsh clothes and withdraw from any material life as an expression of their piety. This can be seen in the manifestation of monasticism. It must be stressed, however, that Islam did not adopt this practice from Christianity. It was perhaps influenced by the early aesthetic-mystical life was found in monasticism and from concepts in eastern Christianity. Nevertheless, the actual manifestation of Islamic mysticism developed along its own lines with its own distinctive Islamic qualities.

By the ninth century, Sufism started to take the direction of change, leading eventually to a practice of asceticism in extreme forms: a spiritual experience understood by those who practice it as a vision into a more real world. From the ninth until the eleventh century, most of the ulema were skeptical about the tradition of mystic personalized piety. However, the teachings and writings of Abu Hamid al-Ghazali (1058 - 1111), one of the leading Muslim jurists who espoused traditional constitutional theories, especially about Sufism, were able in blend Sufi thought into Sunni thought.[40] Although Al-Ghazali himself was a Sufi, his intellectual education made it impossible for him to have a direct Sufi experience although he wrote extensively about ethical mysticism. In all of his writings, it is evident al-Ghazali did not abandon orthodox doctrine. However, he made a conscious effort to introduce Sufi wisdom, his main goal being to revitalize Islam back to its original state. This is illustrated in a section of the twentieth book of *Kitab al-Araba'in*, "The Principles of Following the *Sunna*." Here, al-Ghazali puts forth that it is necessary to follow the path of the Prophet and imitate him in all the things that one does.[41] It was a method of accommodation, enabling Sufi thought to enter into mainstream legal Islam. In other sections of his work, al-Ghazali laid down a foundation for what he believed was correct political power.

Al-Ghazali's writings use the word *siyasa* in the sense it represents a system of organization where people are regulated or governed so they can have their lives enhanced and put in the correct place.[42] This governance is to insure the encouragement of the well-being of people: spiritually, physically, intellectually and morally.[43] According to al-Ghazali, governance is necessary as it assures harmony for the community as a whole. Therefore, a political authority *(sultan* or *imam)* is necessary to control and regulate the people. It is more important to have a person who is a political authority and will be obeyed, thus the manner in which he is chosen is of little importance. The *imam* is necessary because religious order is necessary. This in turns connotes worldly order or the preservation of security of life, livelihood, home and other essentials. All of these orders are related to law and it is therefore the *imam's* responsibility to insure the legal system is obeyed and followed. In essence, religion is the foundation and political authority is the protector. What is completely implicit in this view is that political power is a necessity of life.[44] *Siyasa*, therefore, is not in conflict with *sharia* (Islamic law); it is used normally to clarify it and not supersede it. Al-Ghazali's writings and teachings not only assured the Sufis of a place in mainstream Islam by systematizing clearly and precisely explaining the already existing doctrines, but also demonstrated why Sufism was able to emerge politically.[45]

After al-Ghazali's death, Sufi organizations called *tariqa*. (tariqa: singular; *taruq* or *tariqas*: plural) began to form. Tariqa literally means "the way or the path," and it first connoted a personal form of practicing Islam that was outside of the strict form of the *sharia*. Eventually, those who were practicing Sufis attracted others who would listen, learn and follow what the learned person was teaching. The tariqa, early in its history, was a pragmatic manner of tracing a way of thought, sentiment, and practice for a person who was trying to follow Sufism. It was a way to lead a person through the psychological experiences to find "Divine reality."[46] These groups evolved gradually into loosely organized social groupings, informally gravitating around one particular person who was famous for his teachings, the *shaykh*. The head of a tariqa is usually called a *shaykh* (meaning leader of the prayer carpet), however, in the Sudan many are called *faki*. [47] The teachings of the professed master were able to slowly introduce a method of reflection and release of the soul through mysticism. An important aspect of this experience was a person's experience in a *dhikr*. A *dhikr* used in this reference refers to the frequency that God's name is mentioned. In a group setting, circle, the adherents usually sang hymns, recited specific ritualized intonations that brought them to the edge of a state of ecstasy because of the prescribed methods of body action and breathing. These groups had unusually strong emotional commitments not only to their fellow "brothers" but to the master of the group as well.[48] A Sufi would wander, preaching and teaching to whoever listened to him the "Way," thus generating a following that was the brotherhood.

Starting in the eleventh century, religious hostels (*khanaqahs*)[49] began to play an intrinsic role in the development of the tariqa. The hostels acted as a place for the wandering Sufi to rest while spreading they were in the process of spreading the new devotional message. The *khanaqahs* enabled Islam, particularly Sufism, to spread to non-Arab regions, extending into Africa, Asia and China. By the twelfth century, *khanaqahs* evolved into lavish establishments.[50]

It was during this same period taruq began to organize. The informal groups became more organized and the taruq developed into large organizations based on pious devotional traditions. [51] It was centered mainly around one person who was considered the master. This form of organization was usually far from the diversions of religious hostels. There was no central association for taruq, which are known as brotherhoods, only separate orders spread across the Islamic world. The center of the order was the master, who in essence became the parish. In this instance, it is necessary to conceive of the man as the center and not a place or building, as well as being in essence a parish or a diocese. This is quite different than what is found in other organized religions where a church would be the designated place of organization. Each tariqa became associated with the master, taking its name from the person who founded it, for example: Muhammed 'Uthman al-Mirghani founded the Khatmiyya, which is often called the Mirghaniyya.[52] This practice was not always common place as a tariqa took on the name of a master only when it concentrated on the teachings of one particular person. A brotherhood adopted the name of the master because the rules of life, knowledge and his path to achieve oneness with God, were desired to be perpetuated.[53] Although not all taruq were the same, the pattern followed was similar. In this respect, they were all based on a transmission of esoteric doctrine, rules and methods, which passed through a chain of experts who completed a course of training and received materialization or the presence of the Lord within themselves.

Neo-Sufism

Around the eighteenth century, the nature of some of the tariqa began to change. The tariqa took on a more activist and revivalist form. It was not a change, however, all taruq underwent. There were still some that retained a purely religious association. Those that did change incorporated not only the age-old religious practices, but moved into the political milieu as well. It was the move into a more politically activist mode that actually separated the traditional brotherhood from those of the shifted philosophy. This transition has been termed "neo-Sufism" by the Islamic scholar Fazlur Rahman and has been accepted by other Islamic scholars, such as Nehemia Levtzion and John Voll, who have agreed with the given definition.[54] According to Rahman, Sufism has always been prevalent in reform movements; however, the Sufism that emerged was a transformed one. The medieval doctrines and practices were abandoned and there was a move towards activism. The brotherhoods' original properties did not change as they were still tied to the *dhikr* and centered on one particular leader. However, the major shift now intended the purpose of the *dhikr* to be a union with the Prophet, not God directly. The difference arose because there was a shift among some groups calling for a move away from the esoteric asceticism towards a more fundamental involvement in what was going on in the world. Pre-eighteenth century was marked by loosely structured taruq whereas with the advent of this new expression, the taruq became more organized, concentrating on more correct forms of litanies and practices of the individual group.[55] In view of this new thought, neo-Sufism emerged as highly centralized in its structure and much more concerned with the mobilization of the greater population in order to revive and reform the Islamic society. The tariqa that emerged at this time are referred to as Tariqa Muhammadiyya, taking the name of the Prophet instead of the name of the leader. However, there are certain tariqa of this genre that do have the name of the person who started them, i.e. the Tijaniyya. The devotional aspect changed to one of initiation into an organization. Certain tariqa however, such as the Tijaniyya, demanded strict adherence to the practices and ideas of the brotherhood. The reorganization in those that changed took on a form that was militant and extremely active, expressing the concerns and discontent of the general population to what was wrong with the Islamic world. However, the taruq in this period were not sectarian in themselves. The importance lay in the fact that they had the capacity to turn militant when the need arose. During this period, Sufi teachers made efforts to remove the more ecstatic and pantheistic practices of the Sufi tradition, effecting reform-oriented organization and practices. Most of the leadership of this new wave of thought were scholars who were well versed in the Hadiths[56] and in neo-Sufi thought as well.[57] According, the significance of the activity was one of a widespread mood, instead of being an organized activity or movement.

This evolution of thought was a one that seemed to permeate the Islamic Sufi world at the time. It spread throughout the Islamic world and even branched out into the borderlands and those regions with a Muslim minority. During the nineteenth century, militant movements can be seen occurring in China with the Naqsbandiyya, as well as in black Africa as demonstrated in the Sudan.

3
A History of the Sudanese Sufi Orders through the Khatmiyya

The changes in Sufism not only affected the Arab world, but influenced African Sufism as well. The Sudan, in particular, was one place that underwent transformation. Sudanese Sufism began as the traditional spiritual mystic bonding with Allah. Gradually, the same change towards political activism and expression reached into this region, changing the appearance of the Sudanese Sufi brotherhood. This marked the beginning of adaptability towards modern responses and situations.

Whereas Sufism is a more devotional and mystical experience in other areas of the Islamic world, it has not been the same in black Africa. The black African brotherhood developed as a vehicle for exposing and indoctrinating the masses with the practice of Sunni orthodoxy. In Sahelian Africa, especially the Sudan, Sufis converted the people to a faith that was more personal and more emotional. The acquired faith was much more attached to the love of God than to the fear of him as found in orthodox experiences in other parts of the Arab world. This type of irrational belief appealed to the African people because it was more compatible with their indigenous faiths. Thus, it enabled Sufism to spread more easily throughout Africa. This Sufi orientation is one that is self-critical, flexible, pragmatic and inclusive.

The Islamic faith in the Africa, in general, was, and still

is, a highly popular one retaining much of the customs of the pre-Islamic religions. There is no conflict between following a ritual associated with ethnic or indigenous beliefs as long as the basic belief in Allah is present. This is in direct contrast to the Islam of the ulema and followers of other orthodox beliefs. The African society's basic framework was left in tact, while there was a gradual indoctrination of Islamic ideas to remold and remodel it. What developed was co-existence and mutual accommodation between the indigenous African religion and Islam.[58] Co-existence and accommodation occurred because traditional Islam and Sufism were perceived as being outside the African's intrinsic ethnic beliefs.[59]

Sufism also developed more as a special class cult for dynasties and imperial rule. Those in positions of power merged many of the advantages of Islam with the local animistic practices in order to establish a certain legitimacy among the non-Muslim population. There were no expectations that the words al-Hallaj uttered, have been or will be experienced. Instead, the illiterate masses are taught a basic *dhikr*, which are no more than a few brief lines, in addition to expressing their emotions in a whirling, dizzying personal communication with God (dervishes). In addition, the followers, especially in sub-Saharan Africa, maintain an extremely close link with their religious leader, the latter being the Sufi's intermediary between this world and the next

Islam first entered the Sudan with Nubian traders when they affected a trade treaty with the Arab governor of Egypt in 651-652 AD. As Arab traders always combined trade with proselytization, there was a gradual introduction and acceptance of Islam among the indigenous people. The first lasting conversion in Sudanic Africa occurred, it has been argued, with the Almoravid jihads in the twelfth century, although contact was first established in the seventh century by the Upper Nile and Nubian regions. The Almoravid movement is characterized by the fact many prominent families were converted to Islam during that period. Along with the conversion of leading families, there were mass conversions of their associates as well. It has been contended this was to lessen the difference between the wealthy and their lesser subjects.[60]

The real thrust of Islamization took place in the sixteenth century when holy men were welcomed into the Funj kingdom.[61] During the sixteenth and early seventh centuries, the northern Sudan was dominated by two states: the Funj kingdom with its capital at Sinnar, and Darfur in the west. The Funj kingdom was also known as the Sinnar Sultanate because of its capital city, and at some point was converted completely to Islam. These holy men not only brought Islam to the Sudan but as they were usually adherents of Sufi orders, they introduced Sufism into the Sudan as well.

Sufism was easily accepted in the Sudan in its beginning stages as it was loosely organized. This loose fashion was well suited to the Sudan at the time as it centered only around holy men and their families. These holy men were not only Sufi leaders, but they also taught law and theology, thus fulfilling two roles at the same time. In Sudanese Islam, the melding of Sufi leader and religious teacher occurred. It was not easy to actually make a distinction between the two. One must make a differentiation at this point; normally throughout the Islamic world, in particularly the Ottoman Empire, those who were in the governmental hierarchy of *ulema*, jurists, judges, teachers, were clearly separated from those in the unofficial hierarchy of the Sufi orders. However, in the Sudan, the two seemed to merge together. This can be depicted through the linguistic usage. In black African Sufism, the term *faki* was applied randomly to the holy men. Whether in Islam or Sufism, the colloquial term for a teacher is *faki*. This word is a dialectic form of the stand Arabic word, *fagih*, which means jurist. The plural of *faki* is *fugarā*, which has the basic meaning of dervishes who are members of Sufi orders.[62] These holy men not only acted as agents who transmitted the faith, but they were considered to hold *baraka*, which has been defined as "beneficent force, of divine origin, which causes superabundance in the physical sphere and prosperity and happiness in the physic order".[63] The claim to *baraka* is considered inheritable, thus succession of the *faki* and later the Sufi leader, usually stayed within one family, passing from one generation to another.[64] This rise of an established holy family coming from the relatives of the original Sufi teacher or guide has been characteristic of Sudanese Sufism. According to P. M. Holt, although the main function of the *faki* was to spread the Islamic religion, many possessed great political power, especially those who were local heads of Sufi orders. Idris ibn Arab, a Qadiri teacher, who presumably lived from 1507 to 1651, was supposed to have acted as an oracle to the Funj rulers.[65] Other *fakis* were granted privileges in the form of grants of land and the right to be invested with the symbol of the Funj, which was a stool and turban. One *faki*, Bishara al-Gharbawi, was granted exemption of all taxes and Funj dues, with this being passed down to his successors during the following century.[66] Under the Funj, where there was a weak ruler, many of the *faki'* in fact surpassed the power of the ruler.

Early Tariqa Phase

During the mid-sixteenth century, the first organized tariqas entered the Sudan. They were highly decentralized, with followers surrounding themselves around the teachings of a particular person. Different groupings followed the teachings of a distinct Sufi; each was an autonomous entity with an independent shaykh and independent ritual. In general, these orders were quite small and held a tribal or village connection. The only communality between them was that they held a common connection to the teaching of the founder of the Sufi order.[67] According to accounts, the first major tariqa to be introduced into the Sudan was the Qadiriyya, also called the Jilaniyya, by Taj al-Din al-Bahari.[68] The founding of the Qadiriyya is credited to Abd al Qadir al Jilani in Baghdad in the twelfth century, although there is evidence he never officially started the tariqa himself.[69] It had a very decentralized character, illustrated by the fact that many of the branches/dynasties stemming from it still exist today. The Qadiriyya was especially important as it marked the first introduction of tariqas into the Sudan. It has been associated with a prominent religious family in West Africa, the Kunta. Ahmad al-Bakka'i al-Kunti (d.1504) was considered to be the first major figure from that family to spread his influence which ranged from Timbuktu to as far as the Atlantic Ocean.[70] He was, supposedly, associated very closely with major scholars from Cairo and they introduced scholarly activity with the activities of the Qadiriyya.

The second major tariqa from this period is the Shadhiliyya. The Shadhiliyya, attributed to Shaykh Abu l-Husan al Shadhili (1196-1258), was more of an affiliation than an actual formal tariqa since Shaykh al-Shadhili's followers were never initiated with formal rules or rituals.[71] The first teachings of the Shadhiliyya in the Sudan are attributed to Hammed Abu Dunana in 1445.[72] Similarly to the Qadiriyya, the Shadhiliyya is characteristic of many independent branches, having practically no connection to each other, thus also illustrating its highly decentralized nature. Both are, furthermore, characterized by the fact they are eclectic tariqa, meaning they allowed non-Islamic practices in its rituals in the early stages. It is very significant that Qadiriyya held a very tolerant view of Islamization at its introduction. It accepted many of the local customs and practices that were based on the animistic religion of the indigenous people. Many of the pagan beliefs, saints and customs were incorporated into the local practice of Islam, even adapting them to fit the particular style of Islam that was evolving.

Islam has followed different styles of action within the larger Islamic experience. In order to attract the masses of the people in the Sudan to Islam, many of the tariqa leaders had to be flexible. What this meant was, according to the prominent Islamic scholar, John O. Voll, following an adaptionist style: "a willingness to make adjustments to changing conditions in a pragmatic manner."[73] This made it possible to contend with the challenges facing the Islamic world. In sub-Saharan Africa, even though leaders converted to Islam, the masses did not renounce their traditional faith and practices. Many leaders, likewise, did not give up established conventions holding together societies. What occurred was a religious dualism, which accommodated the traditional values and beliefs while permitting Islam to flourish. Additionally, this religious dualism enabled many of the structures supplying dynamism and social power to the Islamic world to come into effect.[74] The adaptability of many of the Sufi leaders in accepting many of the pre-Islamic practices is indicative of this particular course of action.

Eighteenth-Century Tariqa

By the beginning of the eighteenth century, established holy families began to arise. The family established and associated with a Sufi tariqa surpassed to a large extent the local *fakis*, and the Sudanese tariqa became quite institutionalized. The *fakis* still remained quite influential, although quite overshadowed by established families. Whereas the old form of Sufism still existed in the Sudan, this new type became a dominant feature. The first centralized tariqas were mostly part of a revivalist movement that climaxed during the mid eighteenth to nineteenth century. They arose out of a response to the decaying economic, political and military conditions that existed within the Islamic world. Unlike the Arab reformers who wanted to borrow from Western paradigms,[75] this movement was one which sought to reform from within.[76] The taruq emerged more orthodox as they did not accept many of the accommodating practices that were representative of the old popular wave of Islam. However, the orthodoxy to which they ascribed did not preclude the fact they attracted many adherents.

One of the first tariqa to experience a change at the beginning of the eighteenth century was the Qadiriyya. The Qadiriyya was never a tariqa that had a great following. It spread basically during the revivalist stage in the eighteenth century. Al-Mukhtar al-Kunti (1729-1811) has been credited with the introduction of the Maliki school of Islamic jurisprudence,[77] and with energizing the Qadiriyya throughout the majority of West Africa.[78] The basis for his reviving the brotherhood was organizing ethnic groups and supporters into a enormous confederation, which was able to exert influence in the political, economic and religious sectors, with the main thrust at strengthening Islam.

The principal rival of the Qadiriyya was the Tijaniyya. It was founded in Morocco by Ahmad al-Tijani, then entered into the western Sudan around 1810. The Tijaniyya spread south past the Saharan desert into the Sudan where it was adopted by Moorish maraboutic ethnic groups. This tariqa held an insular characteristic until al-Hajj Umar spread its message by force.[79] The Tijaniyya reflects the neo-Sufi idea that puts more emphasis on a mystical relation with the Prophet than on becoming one with God. The Sultan of Morocco, Suleyman, became involved with this particular faction as he was opposed to many of the older ones. Because of this, there were many government officials who became affiliated with the Tijaniyya.[80] Many of the adherents to this following became very influential in Darfur and northern Kordofan. This group, however, became more interested in trade as towns and markets expanded than they were in providing religious leadership. The Tijaniyya was, notwithstanding, the vehicle through which neo-Sufism was introduced into the Sudan.[81] Both the Qadiriyya and the Tijaniyya had one thing in common; they leaned towards the socio-moral reconstruction manifesting during the eighteenth century: neo-Sufism.

During this period, Sufi teachers made efforts to remove the more ecstatic and pantheistic practices of the Sufi tradition and effect reform-oriented organization and practices. As pointed out earlier, most of the leaders of this new wave of thought were educated both in religious law, as well as the revivalist ideologies. These neo-Sufist ideas arose at the same time another influential movement came about in Saudi Arabia: the Wahhabi. The Wahhabis are more correctly called the Muwahhidun. They are followers of Muhammad ibn Abd al-Wahhab (1703-1792) who established this fundamental order. They too called for strict socio-moral reconstruction that was consistent with the eighteenth century revivalist view. The movement under Ibn Abd al-Wahhab combined religious enthusiasm with militant activity. The movement was able to show Muslims in different areas that military purification was possible. However, many of the revivalist movements emerging during the eighteenth century followed more the lines of the neo-Sufi thought and organization, rather than following the militant ideas of the Wahhabis.

This new thought pattern was particularly prevalent throughout the northern and western Sudan (Islamic Sudan). In this region, the blending of scholarly activities and the Sufi organization was able to produce a foundation of militancy that would become a major theme of Islam in the following century. In many ways, although Islam became part of life, many of the pre-Islamic practices and traditions were kept, creating an adaptionist mixture amenable to many of the local teachers. The southern part of the

Sudan, which was predominantly Nilotic and distinct ethnic groups, however, was not affected. Islamic religious and cultural influence was non-existent until the nineteenth and twentieth centuries when Muslims became quite active in the region with the slave trade. At that point, the southern Sudanese became targets of slave raids in the name of Islam. During the Turko-Egyptian administration,[82] these raids, called *ghazwa*, were waged against non-believers. Many rulers, additionally for their own economic gains, professed that Islam sanctioned slavery.[83] This has led to a fear and continued distrust of the Islamic world.

Revivalist and activist ideas and orders, first espoused by the Tijaniyya, penetrated the Sudan fully by the end of the eighteenth century. One such Sufi order that sprang up in the late eighteenth century was the Sammaniyya. This order arose from the Khalwatiyya which had been founded in Arabia during the fourteenth century. The movement for revival and reform brought a new life to Sufi orders like the Khalwatiyya, and missionaries were sent to Africa to advance those particular teachings. One such missionary, Muhammed ibn Abd al-Karim al-Sammani (1718-1775) established the new sub-order which was named after him, the Sammaniyya. The Sammaniyya was brought to the Sudan around 1810 by Ahmad al-Tayyib al-Bashir.[84] Under his tutelage, a new Sufi philosophy formed, instilling a new vitality into Sudanese Sufism. Noticing the Qadiriyya and other taruq were at a low point, he convinced other leaders into joining with him to revitalize the Sufi movement. For the first time in the Sudan, the Sammaniyya offered a hierarchical structure, which surpassed that of the local religious leaders. Each region had its own *shaykh*, who was able to rally around him the tribes of the region. Ahmad al-Tayyib as one of the major *shaykhs* was quite successful in winning over many of the rich and influential families in each group. Thus, membership in the tariqa spread rapidly. However, this was not long lasting and after al-Tayyib's death, the tariqa split into two separate orders. A further split occurred, breaking the Sammaniyya into three separate branches, displaying the regionalization and fragmentation which was occurring in the order. Only one of these branches, the Tayyibiyya Sammaniyya Bakriyya, had any success in the Sudan.[85] This fragmentation would later play an important role. Two sub-branches, one dominated by the al-Tayyib family and the other by the *Shaykh* al-Quarashi wad al-Zein of the al-Tayyiba near Masallamiya on the Blue Nile, became staunch rivals.[86] The rivalry of the two taruq was indicative of the divisions of loyalty occurring when the Mahdist state came into existence.

Along with the Sammaniyya, another tariqa, despite being quite fractured, had importance in the Sudan: the Idrisiyya. Started by Ahmad ibn Idris, known as al-Fasi, the Idrisiyya did not have the same staying power as other brotherhoods of its kind. His students, known as *al-madrasa al-Idrisiyya* (the Idrisiyya school) were extremely influential especially in the Sudan. When al-Fasi died, many of his followers were instrumental in establishing several Sudanese orders, in particular his principle students, Muhammed 'Uthman al-Mirghani and Muhammed al-Sanusi.[87]

The Khatmiyya

Muhammed 'Uthman al-Mirghani was the first to bring al-Fasi's teachings to the Sudan. Before joining the Idrisiyya, Mirghani joined several different orders: the Naqsbandiyya, Qadiriyya, Shadhiliyya, the Junaydiyya, and Mirghaniyya. At one point he seems to have founded an order of his own, calling it "the seal of the paths" - Khatim al-Turuq - thus, Khatmiyya or Mirghaniyya. Although, according to Ali Salih Karrar, the point at which the Khatmiyya became an independent order is of obscure origin. Reports have al-Mirghani initiating followers into "his way," without naming a particular way, making clear that he was a student of Ibn Idris. Karrar points out that throughout the relationship of Ibn Idris and al-Mirghani, there was no mention of the Khatmiyya as an independent Sufi order. It is known, however, on al-Mirghani's last visit to the Sudan before he joined Ibn Idris in Mecca, he designated his son, Hasan, to be his representative in the Sudan.[88]

The majority of al-Mirghani's influence was felt in the Shayqiyya region.[89] Although he never visited the region, his teachings were communicated by a host of representatives gathered from influential holy clans and religious families. These holy families organized their followers into centers of learning, which were then absorbed into the tariqa's network. It was from these centers al-Mirghani's message was spread. The centers had no problem spreading the Khatmiyya's way especially as al-Mirghani was an extremely charismatic person. According to Ali Karrar, several factors attributed to Mirghani's success: his personality, his scholarly background, his abilities as a Sufi, and the beliefs he taught. Additionally, the way in which he treated other holy men and his followers attracted many adherents. He set rules and disciplines that were not hard to follow, nor magnified by dress or association with the dervishes (*taqashshuf*).[90] One must not overlook, furthermore that there were those who aligned themselves with him as they felt they could receive a more advanced education in the teachings of his mentor, Ibn Idris.[91] Many who joined the tariqa were comparatively comfortable economically. Because of that, they were seeking to consolidate their position against those political elites who were not of the same orthodoxy.

When Muhammed 'Uthman al-Mirghani died, leadership in the Sudan was passed on to his son, Hasan b. Muhammed 'Uthman al-Mirghani(1819-1869). Hasan continued the work his father started. He consolidated the Khatmiyya, which had broken into four regional branches. One of the successes that can be attributed to the Mirghani family was that it was quite successful in keeping the various branches of the Khatmiyya under one central organization. There was only one exception to this: the Isma'il ibn Abdallah at El-Obeyed in the Korodofan province of the eastern Sudan.[92] Each was assigned its own head, especially in the northern and eastern part of the Sudan.[93] The internal structure of the tariqa, which his father set up, was kept in place. It was pyramidal in form with the Mirghani family at the top. As explained in the previous chapter, the leader is an inheritable position based on *baraka*.

The neo-Sufi taruq rapidly developed an organizational hierarchy in the Sudan at the advent of the Turko-Egyptian administration. Although each differed with the names and positions established within each order, they all held a common ground in that all were headed by a *shaykh*. This was the case not only in the new organizational structure that evolved, but was in keeping with the original taruq from the early Islamic phase. The shaykh was the original founder of the path, or the inheritor of the tariqa (*shaykh al-sajjada*)[94] who would guarantee entrance into paradise for his followers. He was considered to possess divine qualities and therefore teach his people how to achieve their desired spiritual goals. Because of his guidance and divine authority, he was given absolute respect and control over the lives of his followers. In the Khatmiyya, the founder, however, was never called a shaykh.[95] Al-Mirghani was usually referred to as *al-imam, al-sayyid, al-khatim*.[96] Not even his son, Hasan, was called shaykh after he succeeded his father. Those who attained the position of *shaykh al-sajjada* did not necessarily inherit it from a direct ascendancy. Succession was spiritual, however it was normally achieved through lineal descent. In the case of the Khatmiyya, as stated previously, only the Mirghani family maintained control of the tariqa. Even the various branches were headed by someone directly from the Mirghani family or through marriage. This chain of command consolidated the various branches of the tariqa, in addition to maintaining the same doctrines throughout each regional branch, and keeping the organizational structure centered around the Mirghani family.

Al-Mirghani recognized three different levels of shaykhs. The first and highest position, *shaykh al- tahqiq*, was the person who reached complete spiritual truth. It is this person who was qualified to direct those who wanted to attain this state. The second grade was *shaykh al-tabarruk*. This was a title al-Mirghani gave to those who were his direct agents and received the right of *baraka* from him. According to al-Mirghani, those in that position were not actually *shaykhs*, but had different titles corresponding to their position in the hierarchy of the tariqa. He emphasized they should not permit anyone to call them a shaykh; they must seek divine assistance from only the leader of the tariqa; and if his instructions were not followed they could be excluded from the order. The final classification was of *shaykh al-qira'a*, which was either a teacher of the Qur'an or Islamic sciences. The person in this capacity was only allowed to give instruction in the Qur'an, and not touch on any part of Sufism. Under these positions, there were the various heads of the different branches of the order. Al-Mirghani gave them all different titles aside from using that of *shaykh*.

In the hierarchy of all Sufi taruq, there were titles given to those who were immediately under the *shaykh*. The most common title is that of *khalifas* or *muqaddams*, meaning of deputy. This is usually given by the head of the order to those who showed complete devotion, gave material assistance and helped spread the order. Each *khalifa* was assigned a district or region that he was responsible for and charged with a diversity of duties. First and foremost, they were the link between the followers and the head of the tariqa. They also were responsible for the rituals and ceremonies in their respective villages, campaign for the order's candidates in national and local elections, along with a myriad of other functions. There was in fact no limit to the duties that a *khalifa* is required to perform.⁹⁷ In the Khatmiyya, the position directly under that of *shaykh* was *na'ib* (deputy). His position in the order was the most important one in that he assisted the *shaykh* with all the management. The *khalifa* in the Khatmiyya was directly under the position of *na'ib*.⁹⁸ There was one who was chosen to be in charge of higher than all of the others: the *khalifat al-khulafa*, meaning chief deputy.⁹⁹ This person was very much the chief administrator of all the *khalifas*. He was the one who settled problems and held the authority to expel a follower not showing the proper respect to his direct *khalifa*. Within the hierarchical organization, the position of *amin* (*umana*, pl.) followed that of the *khalifas*. This standing was restricted to the concern of religious matters. They even had the ability to scrutinize the religious practices of the *khalifat al-khulafa*. If it was found that one was negligent in religious duties, they would be reported directly to the head of the Khatmiyya. Because of their investigatory power, they actually had more prominence within the organization than the *khalifa*.

As stated before, in all taruq, the position of *muqaddam* existed. In many of the taruq, this position was equal to that of the *khalifa* or just under it.¹⁰⁰ Each tariqa had its own definition of the position and responsibilities that the title carried. In the Khatmiyya, this rank was one of a solely administrative type. The *muqaddam* was not permitted to partake in religious undertakings, only to insure visitors to the tariqa were made comfortable. Moving down the ladder of the hierarchy was an office al-Mirghani created himself. This was the *naqib*. Karrar claimed that this office was patterned on a parallelism to the twelve *naqibs* the Prophet chose from amongst his followers in Medina.¹⁰¹ They were charged with the task of arranging the daily religious rituals and making sure the followers observed the devotions.

One other position that was unique in the Khatmiyya was that of the *hakim* (sing. *hukkam*, pl.) This title, which connotes "judge," was accorded those who gave legal advice to followers and was involved in settling disputes. It is similar to a lawyer or even a legal mediator. There were additionally a variety of other offices continuing down the organizational ranks. There were those who were responsible for the mosque; those in charge of the shrines; those who were charged with the job of collecting gifts from the followers. The former could also be women. It was not unheard of in Sudanese Sufism, to find women active in a tariqa. In the Khatmiyya, especially, female members of the al-Mirghani family sometimes held very important roles. Each tariqa, as shown with the Khatmiyya, had their own positions, particular to themselves. In order to distinguish among the ranks, one would have to make a study of each order as they differ from order to order.

The members of the brotherhoods fell into two different categories: the professed and the lay affiliates.[102] This type of membership was not only characteristic of the Khatmiyya, but is found in all taruq. Those who were of the 'professed' group were known commonly throughout the Islamic world as *fuqara* or dervishes. According to Trimmingham, *fuqara* (pl., *faqir*, sl.) means 'a poor one' who is at God's mercy. Although brotherhoods frowned on begging in public, the term is usually associated with that. However, the majority's institution took care of their material needs, with them existing on bequests given over to the order. Additionally, they often lived by whatever they could produce by their own abilities.[103] They formed a very small part of the membership.

In the Khatmiyya, the 'professed' were divided into two groups: *al-khawass*, meaning the "elect", and *khawass al-khawaww*, meaning the "elect of the elect."[104] These two groups usually lived within the tariqa confines, and were taken care of by the general body of followers, who are the lay members. All of the membership was subject to a variety of rules that controlled all aspects of their lives as well as defining their relations with outsiders.[105] It was these rules that provided a certain cohesiveness to the membership and community, enabling them to assert themselves when it was necessary.

The most conspicuous feature of the Khatmiyya was, and still is, the incredible status of the Mirghani family. Only members of the al-Mirghani family are permitted to head the tariqa, with the various branches headed by members of the Mirghani family, either directly or by marriage. Once initiated into the tariqa, it is strictly forbidden for a member to claim any membership to another, except for one exception: the Isma'iliyya in Kordofan.[106] An important aspect of the Khatmiyya's success lay in the fact that it was extremely tolerant of other Sufi orders. Followers were permitted to visit and esteem other Sufi shaykhs. However, loyalty to the order is demanded. Loyalty guarantees reaching paradise for its adherents. There is an extremely tight centralized control over all the various branches coming from the original order. Because of its internal organization, the Khatmiyya became the most politically oriented and powerful tariqa in eastern Sudan. Additionally, the Mirghani family has been able to keep a tight control, both religiously and politically, over the order because of the great wealth they acquired, not only for themselves, but for the tariqa as well. As stated before, a good amount of its members were economically comfortable, having sufficient resources of which a portion was donated to the tariqa. Also, many people from other taruq joined in with him, especially those who were members of the Qadiriyya, and relations were also cemented between the Sammaniyya tariqa.[107]

Furthermore, it is equally significant that Islam, especially as practiced by the Mirghanis, was able to successfully blend and soften legalism with mysticism. Religious leaders combined three major roles in Islam into one: jurisconsult (*faqih*), Sufi (*faqir*), and Qu'ran teacher (*mu'allim*). These were all under one heading, *feki* and the establishment where all these function took place was the retreat (*khalwa*). According to J. S. Trimmingham, "no stress was placed upon ascetic and mystical practice and teaching, but complete reliance on the Mirghanis..."[108] This is not to say family and tribal orders were usurped. These continued to survive and maintain the same vitality as before.

The tradition of combining three roles into one, *feki*, and the blending of legalism with mysticism was undermined quite a lot in 1820 when the Turko-Egyptian invaders established themselves in the Sudan (1820-1885). This aided in the spread of the Khatmiyya, especially in the Shayqiyya region. The Turko-Egyptian regime headed by Muhammed Ali in Cairo brought to the Sudan the idea of organizing a modern state, which would maximize resources for efficiency and extraction. In order to do this, the foreign administration intended to regulate the affairs of everyone under their rule to insure gaining surpluses for their own treasury. When the Turko-Egyptian rule began, Hasan instituted close ties with them.[109] This marked a move into the political arena of a major Sufi order. It was better to cooperate with the foreign authorities than to oppose them. The tariqa acted as an mediator between its followers and the governmental structures in place. It collected taxes, announced decrees, and many of the followers served in the armed forces. In fact, the foundation laid by the Khatmiyya in establishing sympathetic relations with Egypt during the Turko-Egyptian rule has lasted until the present.[110] When Egypt invaded the Sudan, the Khatmiyya cemented ties with the Turko-Egyptian administration which additionally marked the path that they would follow in the political arena: one of adaptability and reconciliation. In order to exercise its political influence, the Khatmiyya did not advocate revolt, but worked from within the administration to accomplish what it desired. It was adaptionist in its political activities, and did not depart from the intellectual foundations of its founder.[111] The Khatmiyya was actually aided in the consolidation of their political influence by the more centralized Turko-Egyptian regime as it cooperated with them, rather than stirring up opposition.

The Khatmiyya was able to acquire political influence because they were able to work as intermediaries between the government and their followers. One of the major reasons Sufi orders were able to act as go-betweens was because the head of the order is the representative and authority for those who follow him in this world and the hereafter. In addition to acting as an intermediary, the Shayqiyya had some of its tribe in the employment of the government.[112] They acted as tax collectors and entered into the army. Because of the relation of the three groups: the Khatmiyya, the Turko-Egyptian administration and the Shaqiyya, it was in the best interest of all three to work and support each other to preserve their own individual authority. This is not to say that the relations between all three were always amicable. There was tension at times between the Shayqiyya and the Khatmiyya, and also between the Turko-Egyptian regime and the Khatmiyya.

Opposition to Turko-Egyptian rule did not appear until the end of the nineteenth century. Discontent with the occupying forces had been brewing under the surface since the original invasion. First of all, the violence that accompanied the original invasion left many with a bitter taste and a desire for revenge. Secondly, inequitable taxation levied by force and increased by illegal demands of various government officials left many people enraged at the Turko-Egyptian regime. There was also a discontent and jealousy on the part of other religious and social groups over the favoritism shown towards the Khatmiyya and the Shaqiyya.[113] Perhaps the most immediate and suppressive cause came from the foreign administration's attempt to curtail the slave trade that was an integral part of the Sudanese domestic and agrarian economy, in addition to being a source of great wealth for the people.[114] This dislocation of economics, political inefficiency, coupled with the growing slave trade from the south contributed to the increased discontent fermenting throughout Sudanese society. Sufi leaders were the ones to voice the unrest the best. Those of the older and more established taruq found their authority was challenged by the establishment of formal sharia courts run by Egyptian *qadis*, along with the central government taking charge of local education.[115] In essence, even though the Turko-Egyptian regime was conciliatory towards the taruq, supporting their local *khalwas*, taruq prestige was greatly diminished. The Egyptians replaced most of the *fakis* with *ulema* (pl., religious scholars, sing. *alim*), and made access to Egyptian education much easier for the Sudanese. This threatened the indigenous education in the Sudan as it sought to replace it with the more rigorous and authoritative Islamic one found at the al-Azhar University in Cairo.[116] The only tariqa not affected by this move was the Khatmiyya because of its close ties with the foreign administration. The Sammaniyya tariqa, however, would play an integral part in militant expression of unrest that followed. The problems caused by the foreign rule mounted over time. The changes had a dramatic effect on the local population whether they were elites or not. The economy, society and lives in general were open to interference by an administration that wanted total control and compliance to the order they established. The main problem was the Turko-Egyptian administration could not provide a rationale to the Sudanese of why they should accept any change in their existing way of life. Moreover, the sentiment was turning to the belief that the impositions of the Turko-Egyptian regime outweighed any benefit derived. Egypt itself was unable to stop the mounting tensions. Its own government was in serious trouble, beset with financial difficulties.[117] All of these issues were going to unite many of the Sufi taruq into a coalition to achieve an independent status of their own.

From the advent of Islam into the Sudan until the end of the Turko-Egyptian administration, it is explicitly clear that

Sufi brotherhoods would follow a path of political activism. The involvement of prominent *faki* in the Funj court illustrates the beginning of Sufi adeptness in gathering a significant amount of power. As holy families began to take shape and rise in standing, political involvement further evolved and was strengthened. The structured taruq therefore provided the vehicle in which political power was consolidated and manipulated in order to achieve express goals. With the arrival of neo-Sufism, the posture of Sudanese taruq further changed to one where rebellion and Islamic nationalism would emerge. The political path of Sufi brotherhoods began to make its mark in Sudan's public arena.

4
The Mahdiyya[118]

In 1881, a movement arose in the Sudan that was revivalist in nature: Mahdism. Throughout the Islamic world, it has been prevalent to find the notion a mahdi, "the awaited guide in the right path" (messiah), would appear. In Islam, there is a widespread belief among both Sunni and Shiites alike of messianic expectancy. A person would arrive who would bring a time of justice and peace without any oppression. This person, the Mahdi, would be a rightly guided leader and rid the world of the existing injustices. The awaited person would overthrow the old order and establish a new theocracy. For the Sunni Muslim, the belief is rooted in the historical tradition of the Prophet and the four 'Rightly Guided Caliphs. This is the only historical period that is customarily accepted without debate by the Sunni community (*umma*), as found in the Sudan. When the Mahdi appeared, the *umma* would re-establish a community based on the Qur'an and the *sunna*.

The movement that occurred in the Sudan, the Mahdiyya, was not Sufi in nature, although it has been compared with that of an tariqa. What is important to understand is that was not at all a tariqa in the traditional pattern. The Mahdiyya resembled that of a tariqa because its founder was associated with the Sammaniyya, thus attracting many other Sufi followers from a diverse amount of orders. From its onset, the Mahdiyya was both a religious and political movement. It was started in June 1881 by Muhammad Ahmad ibn 'Abdallah (1848-1885) who sent out letters informing the important leaders of the Sudan he was the Mahdi.[119] His message put forth since he was the messenger of God and the representative of the Prophet Mohammed, he was going to establish Islam as a global religion, bringing justice and equity to the world.[120] This Sudanese Mahdism professed to contain many of the same elements found in the period of the Prophet and the four Caliphs (*khalifas*, pl. *khalifa*, sing.) of a pure and unadulterated Islam. It was a message that appealed to many in the Sudan as the concept was not new. The expectation of a mahdi appearing predated Mohammed Ahmad's declaration. In order to validate his claim, he likened his flight (*hijra*) to the western region of the Sudan to the flight of the Prophet when he fled to Medina to escape his adversaries. Not only was his flight similar to the Prophet, but the fact that he called for jihad can be reminiscent of the Prophet's call to force all non-believers, whether they be corrupt Muslims, Christians, or animists, into following the creeds and ways he put forth. Additionally, in the fashion of the Prophet, Mohammed Ahmad chose four to succeed him, and called his followers: the Ansar.[121] The familiar path, originally followed by the Prophet, was also manifested by his claims to have had visions in which the Prophet spoke with him. It was these visionary assertions that ultimately transformed Muhammed Ahmad into a *imam* instead of a Sufi *shaykh*. His call to jihad, however, actually meant he was going to dismantle the existing Turko-Egyptian regime and establish a Mahdist state. Muhammed Ahmad was very successful in this sense of using religion to galvanize a strong religious and political reaction. He had a clear nexus as to what he wanted to accomplish religiously and politically.

Sufism played an integral part of the acceptance of Mohammed Ahmad as the expected mahdi. He was an important shaykh of one of the branches of the Sammaniyya, which as stated earlier was the first of the centralized taruq to enter the Sudan. This however, did not seem to be a sufficient role for him to carry out what he desired.[122] Being a Sufi shaykh put Ahmad in the position of being just one of many others, therefore he had to contend with all the competition that arose between the different orders and their respective branches.

Upon his declaration of being the Mahdi, he requested the heads of the other orders to unite in following him. This automatically put him above those who were asked to join with him, and additionally gave him an aura of authority. Many of the *shaykhs* and holy families joined in with him because of his Sufi connections. Their association with him was additionally coupled with the belief that the activist form of Sufism espoused would help them to get rid of the Turko-Egyptian regime and the administrative *ulema* (religious scholars)[123] connected to them. The *ulema* were from Egypt and not a part of the Sufi network that played such an integral part of the acceptance of Sufi political involvement in the Sudan. At first, the Turko-Egyptian regime did not take Ahmad's message very seriously.[124] The *ulema* did voice uncompromising opposition to the assertion of his being a mahdi. They pointed out he did not have the prescribed qualifying factors described in the tradition of mahdism. However, all the discrediting fell on deaf ears, and the *ulema* were consequently considered to be an enemy and cohorts of the Turko-Egyptian regime. In the four years following Muhammed Ahmad's declaration of being the Mahdi, the very primitively armed Ansar was able to completely crush the occupying forces.

Most of the original neo-Sufi orders joined in with Muhammed Ahmad, although not all at once. He started out having the support of the Sammaniyya, and sought the endorsement the Isma'iliyya, Tijaniyya, Majdhubiyya and Khatmiyya. The different brotherhoods would guarantee him success with the different tribal groups in the different regions.[125] The Isma'iliyya and Tijaniyya would give him the support necessary in the western region of the country. At the same time, the Mujdhubiyya would enable him to gain the support of the Beja followers in the Red Sea hills.[126] The Khatmiyya was of particular importance to him because they were the largest and most influential tariqa, having the majority of its support in the urban centers of the riverein region. However, the Khatmiyya did not join in the support of Muhammed Ahmad's Mahdist revolution. This was not surprising since the founders of both groups claimed to have revelations from God.[127] Moreover, the Khatmiyya was not inclined to give up its position of favoritism with the foreign regime, and many of their followers' interests, economically and socially, were intrinsically linked with the Turko-Egyptian administration. Ultimately the leaders of the Khatmiyya were forced into exile in Egypt until the collapse of the Mahdist state.

Those who did throw their support to the Mahdi fell into three categories. There were the truly religious followers from his tariqa who had been with him for many years. These religious followers believed the Mahdi could deliver them from the depravation they conceived to be part of the Sudanese society. It was not actually the Turko-Egyptian administration they were against. They were against any form of government that did not rule by strict Islamic law.[128] They had already experienced certain pressures under the Turko-Egyptian regime. The Egyptian administration brought in established *ulema*, which completely undermined all the authority of the local *fakis*. Their judicial powers were partially given over to the *ulema* as the Egyptians established formal *sharia* courts headed by their own *qadis*, and their prestige diminished radically. Local education moved from being the concern of the *fakis* to the central government.[129] This not only created tension between the administrations, but moreover between the two religious groups. Second, there were those who thought they had something to gain followed the

Mahdi. Then, there was the category of those who suffered under the previous administration, thus throwing their lot in with him as well. This group also contained religious leaders, as well as certain tribal associations. The various tribes and their chiefs were tired of enduring the Egyptian policy of reducing their authority and subjecting them to the general administration of the land.[130] The policies of the joint administration greatly affected them, either indirectly or directly. Many were connected to the lucrative slave trade in the south. The policy, established in 1877, outlawing the slave trade directly affected their livelihood. They actually did not join in the beginning of the revolution, but waited until the Mahdist's forces had taken over Khartoum as the capital.[131] Since they were not particularly religious, this group found that if they used religion as a guise, they would be able to secure their economical and political interests, especially where the slave trade was concerned. To them, it was easier to invoke Islam because slavery was considered acceptable. The third group, nomads of the Baqqara tribes,[132] basically had no other agenda except to rid their country of the hated Turks. This meant they would not have to be controlled by any established government. Being under any established authority was something that ran contrary to everything they believed. A crucial point about the three categories of the followers is they were very much based on tribal organization. It can not be overlooked that tribal affiliations were extremely strong, not only for taruq, but in answering the call to join the Mahdi's revolution.

With so many people dissatisfied with the existing situation under the Turko-Egyptian administration, it is not difficult to understand how Mohammed Ahmad's program was successful. The reaction of the Sudanese people to the Mahdist movement (Mahdiyya) was one to the changes in the political, economical, and religious life under the Turko-Egyptian regime. This is not to say support for the Mahdi was a universal, with only the Khatmiyya refusing to join.

There were other Sufi leaders who hesitated. However, in letters to the various Sufi *shaykhs*, Ahmad let it be known that all who did not join with him in his *jihad* would henceforth be considered an infidel, thus an enemy.[133]

The state instituted by the Mahdi was based on that of the Prophet and the Qur'an. He imposed the *sharia* (Islamic law) in order to cure all the depravities he believed were present in society. The idea behind this was to emphasize uniformity. The major problem that occurred, however, was Muhammed Ahmad actually succeeded in creating discontinuity rather than uniting the Sudanese. In the beginning of his movement, the Mahdi recognized Sufi leaders and their respective taruq as faithful followers. He seemed to be willing to accept there was a group division of authority as long as everyone was ultimately loyal to him. This changed midway into his revolution.

Starting in 1883, intolerance began to grow. Once the Mahdist state was firmly established, it turned against those who had been its staunch supporters, calling for no loyalty except to the Mahdi himself. In a decree issued in 1884, the Mahdist state completely denounced and forbid any association with Sufi orders, demanding complete undivided loyalty to the Mahdiyya.[134] This intolerance could probably have been foreseen. As pointed out by Nicole Grandin, Mohammed Ahmad, before his declaration of being the mahdi, had already committed one of the gravest sins a disciple could do. He outwardly criticized his shaykh for his lack of strict religious observance.[135] Under the rule of absolute submission to one's shaykh, the holder of baraka - a characteristic of Sudanese Sufism - one is considered a heretic when one does not have a shaykh or show respect for his declared shaykh. It is said of that person that "his shaykh is the devil" (*shaykhu Iblis*)..[136] His condemnation of the orders, and consequently his ban on association with them can not be considered as a move out of character. Evidence points to Mohammed Ahmad as using any means he could to make sure that his message was not only accepted but carried out. This condemnation of the Sufi orders became a characteristic of the expanding Mahdist state. It left very little room for local practices and traditions, leading to a degree of ideological and political centralization. The Mahdist state, once in power, called for conformity to its ideals, of which, in the end, many were not willing to follow. It can not be said the Mahdiyya, even though it boasted many followers in the beginning, was representative of the diverse ethnic and religious communities found in the Sudan. An excellent example of this is found amongst the Beja people. Initially the Beja supported the Mahdiyya, however, once the new central administration was established, they rebelled at being under their control. The Mahdist state went against many of their tribal interests, as well as forcing them to contradict their loyalty to the Khatmiyya. One of the major leaders under the Mahdist state, Osman Digna, found he had to put down successive tribal and sectarian revolts among his own people. The consequences were that by the time of the demise of the Mahdist state, there were few Beja who did support the government.[137]

Those who did follow Muhammed Abdah ibn Abdallah successfully drove out the Turko-Egyptian administration, along with their British allies. By the time Khartoum was captured, the Mahdi and his Ansar held control over the majority of the former Egyptian Sudan. He moved the capital from Khartoum to Omdurman, and set up a primitive administrative government. This was to be his base from where he believed he would conquer the rest of the Muslim world. His belief did not come to pass as he died from a sudden illness on June 22, 1885. At the time of Ahmad's death, the majority of the Sudan had come under his control, and the first fundamentalist rule began. The Sudan became a state that intended to revive Islamic ideas and practices of the original community of Mohammed. At the same time, the Mahdist state can also be considered one of the first modern national entities in Africa.[138]

The government established by the Mahdi, as stated before, was rudimentary, but was fully functional. It was a state that was both powerful and extremely militant. The Mahdist state was organized into three institutions: the supreme command of the Mahdi himself, a financial and a judicial system. As head of the state, the Mahdi possessed an unequaled position because of his proclamation of divine investiture. As he was originally a shaykh in a Sufi order before his proclamation of being the Mahdi, Ahmad retained the practice of declaring an oath of allegiance. In a tariqa, when a person is initiated into the order, an oath of allegiance is uttered between the follower and his shaykh. Although the Mahdi demonstrated intolerance towards Sufi brotherhoods, it was this part of his Sufist heritage he incorporated into his state, requiring his followers to swear their loyalty to him. There are two different versions of the oath, which additionally demonstrates the Mahdi's dedication in following the Prophet's path. One can see in many ways the similarity to the one declared between the Prophet and his followers. The first is the one that was sworn to the Prophet Muhammed, followed by the oath of allegiance to Muhammed Ahmad.

> I have sworn allegiance to God and his apostle, and I have sworn allegiance to the Mahdi, and I have sworn allegiance to this his agent, to follow him, and to establish the Faith, and I have covenanted with God and his Apostle thereupon, an I have sold my possessions and myself to God to aid the Faith, and my possessions and myself are devoted to God.
> We have sworn allegiance to God and his Apostle, and w have sworn allegiance to you, in asserting the unity of God, that we will not associate anyone with him, we will not steal, we will not commit adultery, we will not bring false accusations, and we will not

disobey you in what is lawful. We have sworn allegiance to you in renouncing this world and abandoning it, and being content with that is with God, desiring what is with God and the world to come, and we will not flee from the *jihad*.[139]

The inclusion of the Sufist oath of allegiance into the state has been one of the main reasons the Mahdiyya has been compared with a Sufi brotherhood.

The Mahdi's rule was one that was characterized by all decisions being made solely by him. During the time he was in command, he never gave up control to any of his high officials. He alone exercised the right of establishing all rules and laws within his state, even though he did delegate responsibility to others to carry out his proclamations. His rules and regulations were not issued without any advice whatsoever. Although he never organized an advisory council, he did seek counsel from his *khalifas* and other important people within his regime. Naum Shoucair's research has shown that upon the fall of Khartoum, Muhammed Ahmad set up an administrative council. However, the council did not really function as such and was dissolved by his successor.[140]

Directly under the Mahdi in his chain of command were his three appointed *Khalifas* (caliphs).[141] The three *khalifas* were associated with the three principle followers of the Prophet. As stated earlier on in the chapter, the Mahdi had chosen four people to follow him: the Ansar.[142] Despite being chosen to follow Ahmad, their titles were not given to them until after the establishment of the state. All three held titles that were the same as three of the four principles associated with Muhammed. Abdallah ibn Muhammed was first *khalifa* – *Khalifat al-Saddiq*- after Abu Bakr. He was the direct successor to the Mahdi and took command upon his death in 1885. The other two were the *Khalifat al-Faruq*—Successor of Umar—and *Khalifat al-Karrar*—Successor of Ali

(Muhammed's cousin). The fourth position was never filled. These positions were extremely important in the chain of command of the Mahdi as they were not only his successors, but they were in charge of his military as well. Each one was given a command of a military division. The division of the army was one that was tribal in its character. Each division represented a major cultural and tribal division within the Sudan. In many ways, it also encompassed the different Sufi organizations that threw their support behind the Mahdi, as they too held a distinct tribal affiliation.[143] The two major divisions were under *khalifat* Muhammed Sharif, and *khalifat* 'Abdallah al-Ta'ishi, which were named the Red Flag and the Black Flag respectively. They both held the loyalty of the people from two separate regions, *Kalifat* Muhammed Sharif held the loyalty of the people from the region known as the *awlad al-balad*, and *khalifat* 'Abdallah al-Ta'ishi held the loyalty of those who were members of the Baqqara tribes. Thus this led to tension developing between the two camps. The third military division was under *khalifat* Ali ibn Muhammed Hilu, which was titled the Green Flag. The Green Flag was relatively small thus posing no great menace to the political aspirations of the other two political military divisions. However, the political tension of the Black Flag and Red Flag divisions was to an important role in the development of the Mahdist state.

The original followers of the Mahdi as pointed out earlier came from those who were involved with the slave trade in the region of *awlad al-balad*. Most of these people were from *Ja'aliyyin* and *Danaqla* tribes.[144] Many of those chosen to head the military ranks were from that particular group. Once the Baqqara tribes joined in, there was an upset in the balance of power because the military strength of the Black Flag started to surpass that of the Red. Those who followed the Red Flag tried to gain higher positions nearer to the Mahdi based on their previous associations with him. They had been his first supporters and would have remained the most numerous if there had not been the move to the Qadir.[145] However, one particular decree issued by the Mahdi put *khalifat* 'Abdallah in the more powerful position: he conferred unconditional powers on 'Abdallah, naming him his *Khalifat al-Siddiq*. Therefore, the succession and power were assured to 'Abdallah and his followers of the Baqqara tribes.

As in any military organization, there were officers under the *khalifas*. These were usually called *amir*, meaning commander. Those who subordinate to the *amirs* were called *muqqaddams*.[146] This title again shows the parallel to Sufi orders as pointed out in the chapter on the Khatmiyya. Those directly under the *khalifa* in the brotherhood were also given the title of *muqqaddam*. Early in the new administration, the rank and file were known as *darawish*, dervishes. This was term applied to the Ansar in general to signify helpers.[147] However, later on during his administration, the Mahdi forbade use of the term and insisted on having his followers called only the Ansar. However, with the early use of the term *darawish*, one is again drawn to the parallel to Sufi orders.

The Mahdi additionally established a financial system within the state. He appointed a treasurer to safeguard the wealth of the state. The treasury, called *Bayt al-mal* (house of wealth), was designed to contain all the material wealth, both cash and resources, of the new state. According to Holt, it was not an easy task to convince the various tribal members to hand over their resources as they were accustomed to keeping what they had gained from their raids.[148] This was achieved by using the *sharia*: one fifth went to the head of the community and the rest was divided amongst the tribal forces. In the case of the Mahdist state, the remaining four fifths went to the treasury. Taxes were also levied, with this being accomplished also by following the Islamic religion strictly. The tax was in the form of *zakat*. Zakah is one of the Five Pillars of Islam that requires that all Muslims pay a charity tax to the community. This was usually paid in the exchange of goods as the use of currency was unusual except in cities. Coins did circulate in the Mahdist state, but initially, they were from the Ottoman Empire and Egypt. It was not until Khartoum fell to the Mahdist troops that the Mahdi exercised a prerogative of state building: striking money. The coins manufactured by the new state were a gold pound and a silver dollar, with the mint being a subdivision of the newly formed treasury.[149]

The newly formed state additionally had to confront problems of legislation and the enforcement of laws. The Mahdi was the supreme authority over what laws were passed and they were based on the Qur'an and the *Sunna* (way of the Prophet). As he claimed to be reviving the Islamic faith and bringing justice to the world, it was natural that his laws were based on the original laws set down by the Prophet. However, as the head of a new state, other problems arose that could not be solved from the standpoint of the Qur'an. Legislation had to be enacted in order to resolve questions of everyday living. Even though the final law was in the hands of the Mahdi, he delegated powers to various others, such as his *khalifas*, and chief officers. Above all of his judicial administrators, he appointed a chief judge - *qadi al-Islam* - who held the position of being the special delegate of the Mahdi in legal matters. All legal matters were decided by the laws in the *Sharia*, with the Mahdi usually taking the initiative. The title actually was more of a token since all major decisions had to be passed by the Mahdi himself.

For all intents and purposes, the state created by the Mahdi was the first state in Africa to oppose colonial intrusion, and achieve it. It began with a desire to throw out the infidel from the Sudan and developed into a functioning independent country that was based on Islamic ideals. When Muhammed Ahmad died, the state he created did not collapse. The state apparatus was strong enough that his successor *Khalifat* 'Abdallah was able to keep it intact for the next decade. 'Abdallah strengthened the Mahdiyya and an increasingly centralized administration was established. He instituted a more complex financial system, which in many ways took the Sudan back to the hated tax system of the Turko-Egyptians. The power of the judicial system was also increased, but final authority was left in his hands. Although the Mahdist state was besieged by problems, it remained militarily strong and quasi united, requiring a foreign military force to put an end to it. In 1898, Anglo-Egyptian forces captured Khartoum in the Battle of Omdurman. *Khalifat* 'Abdallah was killed the following year in 1899, thus ending the Mahdiyya and putting the Sudan back under foreign rule.

The ideals of the Mahdi nonetheless left a legacy, which would manifest itself in Sudanese politics in the future. The state that had been set up was further proof that Sufi brotherhoods held the ability to become politically active when necessary. The Mahdist state was built through a coalition of brotherhoods, defining a future political role for those who followed the Ansar. The feeling of nationalism first manifested by the Mahdist Revolution would be the earmark of the modern political party, the Ansar, thus confirming the political strength and adaptability.

5
Political Evolution

The political structure and aspirations of both the Khatmiyya and Mahdiyya did not die out with the demise of the Mahdist state. During the nineteenth century, both set into motion the political path they would follow until the present. The Khatmiyya acted as a pseudo government because of the way it was organized. It also established a liaison with the foreign powers that expressed the wishes of its followers, and protected their interests. The Mahdiyya was an actual government, with an internal organization that functioned in holding the Sudan together for a period of time, even if it did not represent all the diverse opinions and interests shared by the Sudanese people. It strength was seen in the fact that it took a foreign power stronger than it to cause its collapse. In the previous chapters, the description of their history, organizational and political structure did not explain why both the Khatmiyya and Mahdiyya became important political entities in the future of the Sudan. Since not all religions have expressed themselves in the political arena, the inherent aspects of Sufi brotherhoods need to be analyzed to fully understand why in the Sudan both taruq were able to sustain their political strength.

Political Islam has been considered a relatively new phenomenon in the Islamic world. In the Sudan, it has been associated with its politics only since the coup led by Omar al-Beshir in 1989.¹⁵⁰ However, this premise is actually quite misleading. Islamic political activism actually started with the advent of the Khatmiyya during the mid-nineteenth century, and then became more pronounced with the Mahdiyya. Their influence remained very significant in the Sudan, with both of them possessing a striking similarity.

Both the Mahdiyya and the Khatmiyya shared one prominent feature; they both were sectarian in character.¹⁵¹ A major aspect of the Sudan's political make-up has been that its internal politics have always been under the influence and dominance of sectarianism since the nineteenth century.¹⁵² Sectarian refers to the religious allegiances that manifested, and still do, during political upheaval and conflict in the Sudan. This sectarianism illustrates a continuing belief and loyalty of the religious orders, not only in the Sudan, but elsewhere in the Islamic world. However, political activism in Islam cannot be considered only a nineteenth century phenomenon, occurring particularly in the Sudan. One can see expressions of it in much of Islamic literature, going back to the Qur'an where the faithful are specifically instructed not to obey any ruler who enjoins them to act in sin.¹⁵³ In the nineteenth century, the activism that started to occur was one of a nationalistic nature.

The majority of the nationalistic movements in the Muslim world have included those from religious groups, whether it be Sufi or others. The first national movement in the Sudan was perpetrated by the Mahdiyya, using religion as a pretext for political protest against the Turko-Egyptian administration. Even the Anglo-Egyptian regime that conquered the Mahdist state, underestimated the power of the zealousness of the Sufi brotherhoods.¹⁵⁴ They believed if they introduced a Western education, a strong secular movement would occur.¹⁵⁵ This, however, proved to be misleading. The sectarian feelings amongst the Sudanese proved to be much stronger.

Political activism and sectarian movements have been,

and are still, associated with responses to an unwanted element, whether it be a colonial power asserting its influence over the colonized or intellectual thought stemming from ideas perpetuated by those who desire change. However, to apply this to the sectarian movements that have appeared throughout Islamic history would be a misrepresentation. These movements actually have been quite characteristic of the Islamic world as they sought to cope with constantly occurring changes.[156] In fact, radical activism, both politically and socially, can be considered as intrinsic in Islam. Although the form of response changes from one area to another, all of the activist movements had a commonality. According to John L. Esposito, in the *Islamic Threat, Myth or Reality*, they all shared

> a sense that existing political, economic, and social systems had failed; a disenchantment with, and at times a rejection of, the West; a quest for identity and greater authenticity; and the conviction that Islam provides a self-sufficient ideology for state and society, a valid alternative to secular nationalism, socialism, and capitalism.[157]

When Muslims perceived their religion had stagnated or failed, many sectarian movements emerged as a method for reestablishing Islamic ideals that had worked in the past. The activism on the part of the Sufi taruq in the Sudan, accordingly, was a twofold reaction: an assault on the colonial presence and a quest to reestablish orthodoxy and clarity to Sudanese Islam.

Authority

The Khatmiyya, under the leadership of Muhammed 'Uthman al-Mirghani, embodied the nineteenth century teachings of his mentor, Ahmad ibn Idris, asserting a unity and solidarity exempt from the tribal fragmentation that previously characterized the Sudanese countryside.[158] The Mahdist state united the majority of the Sudan to rid itself of its colonial presence while calling for a renewal of Islamic purity. However, this was not the only reason for their continued success.

The tightly organized internal structure of both the Khatmiyya and the Mahdiyya was crucial to their political success. It was this internal structure that gave them the impetus to gather a certain amount of political power. As explained previously, each founder of a Sufi order put forth certain rules and obligations concerning the relationship between himself and his followers. He was the person who was the spiritual head of the order and whose righteousness could only be passed on to his descendants.[159] As seen with the Khatmiyya, only members of the al-Mirghani family headed the various centers for the followers in different parts of the country. The shaykhs were the final authority on all religious matters. As head of the tariqa, they are respected for their piousness, along with being respected for their gift of *baraka*. Most of their followers believed them capable of performing miracles (*karama*). It was these two elements combined that gave the shaykh the necessary components to embellish their image and promote their control. A shaykh was not only the spiritual leader of his followers, but he was the secular authority as well. He was not only responsible for the spiritual well being of his community, but serves as the mediator for internal disputes as well as external ones, whether they were in the social or economic framework. The shaykh was the person who acted on behalf of his followers with the local authorities. He was the person who held "sacred authority."[160]

In the Islamic religion, learned scholars, the ulema, hold what can be called "sacred authority." The ulema are the ones who are able to command a certain amount of respect from the people around them, representing certain social and economic interests of the community, as well as being versed in the Qur'an and the law. In Islamic communities, especially one such as the Sudan where the literacy rate and knowledge of the Qur'an are almost nonexistent, those who are versed and educated in the Qur'an and sharia are accorded an enormous amount of respect and authority.[161]

Those who were inevitably in this position were given their authority through hereditary succession. Because of this, it transmitted *baraka* by descent, thus increasing the authority a shaykh and his descendants held with followers. As the Khatmiyya and the Mahdiyya both had the two largest followings, Muhammed Ahmad and al-Mirghani commanded the loyalty of the majority of the people, especially in the rural regions. The control of so many people, which translated into accumulation of material assets, further solidified the authority that the each leader held.[162]

Sufi shaykhs, especially in the rural areas, not only took on the role of the ulema, but extended their influence to represent the groups or their tariqa as a whole. They did this because they were able to command respect, which was important as their recognition gave them their legitimacy.[163] The respect the shaykhs commanded came from the fact that they were considered learned scholars and held a position of prestige within their community and amongst their following. They were the ones who were best able to externalize the values and religious reference points of society. The shaykh in the Sudan was commonly recognized as the principal religious and political figure. Their followers looked to them for preserving Islamic customs, enforcing law, and for guidance in their economic, social and political lives. In Islam, it is not important which title is given to a leader. What is important is that he is the agent or representative of the Muslim community - in this case, the tariqa - to carry out God's orders and execute his laws. In this aspect, the Shaykh's followers trusted him to safeguard both their internal and external securities. According to James Piscatori and Dale Eickelman, this "acquiescence, the involuntary investiture of authority" was only a fraction of the whole. Those with "authority transform themselves over time into 'natural leaders' and, through manipulation of symbols of society and invocation of tradition, made claims of obedience and obligation on others."[164] This was seen through the evolution of the Sufi tariqa and its shaykh, with the shaykhs demanding absolute loyalty of followers even if they themselves belonged to various other taruq. Through the use of the tariqa, and the promise of entrance into paradise by adhering to the proscribed rituals, the Sufi shaykh used tradition to consolidate a "sacred authority." According to Max Weber, this "traditional authority" is based on a belief in the sanctity of tradition, or "which is customary and has always been so, and prescribes obedience to some particular person."[165] It was not a codification of rules. Rather, it rested on the idea the person who was in the position of authority had inherited it or had been vested with it by a much higher authority. It did not matter if those invested with authority were ignorant or learned; it mattered only that they were the accepted "sacred authority." This type of traditional authority can only applied to the Sufi shaykh within the scope of the functionality of the tariqa. Weber further elaborated that personal or traditional authority was also a part of social conduct and, therefore, was a form a patriarchalism. This type of authority came from the time-honored tradition in the Islamic religion that there were those who had the right to authority based on their religious knowledge. More importantly, sacred authority is based on an acceptance and belief by the majority of Muslims that Allah invested certain people with the right to hold that authority.

Even before the advent of Sufi orders, there were relationships between learned masters (shaykh) and those who wanted to learn: the disciple (*faqir*).[166] Those who were the masters were able to trace back through a chain, *silsila*, the knowledge of their masters to Muhammed. What occurred within the relationship of the disciple and the master was a spiritual bond formed, transcending the past and extending even into the future. This bond was one in which the disciple remained a disciple forever, although he may go on to become a master himself. Within this bond was the innate understanding there was a correct discipline and doctrine established.[167] As the Sufi tariqa evolved, those pre-Sufist bonds transferred between the Sufi shaykh and his adherents. The bond further established the authority given to the shaykh and enabled the tariqa to be a strong permanent organization.

The acceptance of the authority of a person who was knowledgeable and able to transmit this knowledge was one even put forth by Muhammed in the Qur'an: "The noblest among you in the eyes of God, is the most pious."[168] In analyzing this statement, it becomes obvious the person who follows the divine commandments of the Prophet is the one who should be obeyed. Sayyid Jamal al-Din al-Afghani asserted the meaning of this phrase quite succinctly: "Whoever surpasses all men in piety, that is to say, in the practice of Islamic law, will be distinguished by respect and veneration accorded to him."[169] Therefore, the Sufi shaykh embodied the ultimate pious figure to his followers, assuming in every aspect the role of leader and enforcing obligations on both on himself as well as his followers.

Leadership and the relationship between those in power and the ruled have been a common topic in Muslim political literature. One of the three basic tenets put forth as to the obligation of the ruler to the ruled was the ruler owed certain obligation to his subjects. According to Bernard Lewis in *The Political Language of Islam*, there was a basic agreement among those versed in Islamic jurisprudence on this specific principle:

> The ruler owes a collective duty to the Islamic community as a whole, to defend its interests, protect it against its enemies, and advance its cause; he also owes a duty to the individual believer, to enable him to live the good Muslim life in this world, and thus prepare himself for the next. In return for these services, he is entitled to command the obedience of his subjects in everything except sin.[170]

Although, Lewis was referring to the ruler of a state in more modern times, it can be easily applied to what is expected and required of the relationship between the shaykh and his followers, within the limits of the Sufi brotherhood. Thus, both shaykh and followers had duties towards each other, which had expectations going along with it.

From the viewpoint of political development, this is very similar to the characteristics identified as necessary in establishing modern political leadership. Those who assume the role of leadership must be sensitive and embody the quintessential essence of their community or society. Leaders must be aware of what values to preserve while at the same time moving their populace in the direction of effectiveness.[171] What this means is leaders must give their communities an awareness of what is happening around them in the political world. With awareness, a community is best able to express acquiescence or opposition to particular ideas. Then, in undertaking the role as a leader, the leader must manifest the principles of his constituent. In the case of the Sufi tariqa, the shaykh must hold his community together by being sensitive to their needs, spiritually and secularly. In return, followers give him full obedience.

Followers, once initiated into the tariqa, were assured of preferential entry to paradise at the price of unquestioning submission to the shaykh. In the Sudan, as in other African states, grassroots Islam tended to be inspired more by Sufi leaders than by intellectuals.[172] Followers came from many different regions and joined orders because their parents or grandparents before them did. It is a social custom and practice of the people and the majority of the illiterate masses join.

This convention had its foundations in the advent of Islam in Africa. Early Islamic clergy were able to draw their communities into the Islamic religion because they were familiar with their local languages and practices. They were able to allegorize lessons from the Quran and the *Hadiths* by drawing upon images of indigenous customs and histories. Individuals would join because they would be part of the larger community. Holding this did not negate a belief in God, but having a communal identity has been an essential part of African heritage. Because of this grassroots phenomenon, the literate elite had the opportunity to manipulate religion for their purposes, whether it be in the best interests of their followers or not. Elites were able to strategize to get their followers to adapt to changing realities, politically and economically. In essence, the follower was protected in many ways from the disruptive impact of the modern state by not having to have to deal with it on a daily basis. This was consistent with the expected relationship between the ruler and the ruled: an acceptance of manipulation and protection, with protection primarily being perceived.

This authority handed to the Sufi Shaykh lasted throughout his life, and then it was inherited by his followers in the form of the institutionalized tariqa. The tariqa derived its strength or political power from the fact that if it supported a particular goal or political movement, it was quite effective in influencing the outcome.[173] Additionally, funding within taruq played an intrinsic part in the ability to express a variety of political concerns. Many shaykhs with large followings gained great prestige because their wealthy followers donated large sums of money as charitable bequests. They not only acquired great wealth through gifts, but they were able to gain assets by controlling trade routes and agriculture. This funding made, and still makes it possible for a variety of expressions to be heard.

By virtue of the institutionalized and centralized characteristics, tariqas are not and cannot be apolitical. Not all Sufi orders are highly centralized throughout the Islamic world. However, in Africa and the Sudan in particular, one can accept the concept of a highly organized an centralized order. Sufi orders have enough power within their own groups to challenge the state's right to speak for Islam. In addition, they become extremely influential as many of the *ulema* belong to them. In the Sudan, a prime example of this was Muhammed Ahmad. As pointed out earlier, Ahmad mobilized many of the tariqas into supporting his contention that he was the Mahdi because of his own personal involvement in the Sammaniyya. His involvement as a traditional authority in the Sammaniyya automatically gave him a legitimacy amongst those who followed him.

Nevertheless, this alone did not give Muhammed Ahmad the legitimacy needed to galvanize such a large response to his assertion he was the Mahdi. Those who followed Ahmad did so because of his religious power, in addition to answering the underlying desire to overthrow the Turko-Egyptian regime. Al-Afghani in his treatise on Islamic solidarity put forth:

> If among the Muslims one found a minor ruler of whatever racial origin, who followed divine commandments, was zealous in applying them, compelled the people to apply punishments which they ordain, obeyed the law himself like his subjects, and gave up trying to distinguish himself through vain pomp, it would be possible for this ruler to enjoy widespread power and great influence. He could assume great authority in Muslim-inhabited countries. He would not encounter great difficulties in doing this, for he would not have to spend money, or build

up his army, or conclude alliances with the great powers, or seek the assistance of partisans of civilization and freedom. . . . He could accomplish all this by following the example of the orthodox caliphs (the early caliphs of seventh century Islam), and by returning to the original sources of Islamic religious law. His conduct would bring a revival of strength and a renewal of the prerequisites of power.[174]

Al-Afghani's assertion not only legitimizes the stance that Ahmad took, but it was exactly the path he followed in proclaiming himself the Mahdi. Again, the authority Muhammed Ahmad claimed was supported as he represented the majority of the Sudanese Muslims in their immediate need to return to a more orthodox Islam and rid themselves of the foreign presence. Neo-Sufist thought had affected the majority of Sudanese Muslims through their involvement in taruq, therefore they were quite aware of the prevailing attitude to return to an orthodox position. Additionally, they could not help but be aware of the Turko-Egyptian administration in their country, which was unacceptable to them.

In many ways, Ahmad mobilized people to follow him because he held the qualities of charismatic authority. This is different from the traditional authority a Sufi shaykh had vested in him. Charismatic authority is based on a specific individual and the command given to given has no rational reason or rule nor does it rest upon tradition.[175] It is based on the desire of people to put their trust in someone whom they feel will advance their goals, especially in the midst of a social crisis. The discontent with the Turko-Egyptian rule was not only having an alien presence in command, but moreover in the social upheaval the Egyptian *qadis* caused by usurping power from the local religious leaders. Part of the charismatic authority Ahmad held came from the fact he was a Sufi shaykh. Donal Cruise O'Brien has asserted that perhaps the charismatic authority held by a figure such as Muhammed Ahmad was due in part to the fact he was considered to be endowed with *baraka*. However, O'Brien does admit that *baraka* is not charisma.[176] As *baraka* is usually considered inherited, it seems that it is more fitting to attribute this to traditional authority.[177] Traditional authority is one that is usually recognized and accepted as being inherited, handed down in a line of succession. The concept of working miracles can be considered as a charismatic force; however, the type or quality of the miracle must be taken into consideration. In the case of a charismatic authority, it is not a miracle of divine nature, but rather one that will cause a social change. Muhammed Ahmad, in his contention that he was the Mahdi, was not only stating that he was blessed with a divine presence, he was offering to the Sudanese Muslim a chance to rid themselves of an undesired occupancy. This ability of promising a restructuring of a collapsed social order, where those values considered intrinsic to the wellbeing of people were perceived destroyed, also gave Ahmad the authority he needed. To the masses that initially followed him, he embodied the ability to provide a continuity and coherence, especially in reestablishing a network of social recognition and improvement.[178] As pointed out in an earlier chapter, this element was of crucial importance to the followers of Sufi orders. It was this sense of crisis that gave Muhammed Ahmad the charismatic authority needed to be listened to. He was willing to challenge the existing conditions, which up until that point no one had done. Ahmad was from this perspective, a charismatic personality. He was the one who reflected the immediate needs of the Sudanese people. This urgency for immediate change existed in the minds of the Sudanese, consequently Ahmad as a self-proclaimed saint gave a sense of divine authority. He embodied all the elements of his society, which gave him an authority and legitimacy. It is this sense of the divine or sainthood, Max Weber saw as being an important factor in the establishment of charismatic authority.

The Body Politique

Both Muhammed Ahmad and Muhammed Uthman al-Mirghani organized their headquarters in a central place, such as Khartoum with the Khatmiyya, where followers could gain an audience with the spiritual head.[179] The shaykh, by virtue of his religious leanings, tended to withdraw from the outside world. Therefore, his headquarters was a place the rural inhabitants were able to identify with since it was secluded from the every day going on of the city, but central in its accessibility. It was necessary to establish a neutral yet central location as rural followers tended to look at their urban counterparts with both hostility and suspicion.[180] The Sufi tariqa actually offered more to the rural inhabitant than to city dwellers and civil servants. The headquarters, while being the center of the tariqa's religious activities, also served as the bureaucratic center of the order. This bureaucratic organization gave the Sufi order the infrastructure necessary to act in the political arena.

As pointed out in chapter three, the Khatmiyy was organized in an extremely structured fashion. The *khalifas* or *muqaddams* were responsible for the administration of different districts, both religiously and secularly. This indicates the way political parties function on a state or national level. They linked the shaykh with his followers in a daily contact. They were the conduit for binding together the forces of charisma, accountability, organization and ideology together into a larger political culture, even though they were within a religious organization. Because of the functions the *khalifas* performed, they succeeded in giving a sense of citizenship to the members of the tariqa. Each member identified with belonging to a larger body. Because of this, the tariqa acted as a vehicle to organize political participation in political decisions as well as a political party can.[181] Political parties have daily contact with their constituency, enabling them to assert new ideas and mobilize them into action when necessary. The *khalifa* acted as the deputy of the tariqa in carrying out the shaykh's desires. He was in daily contact with followers in his district, involving himself in both religious and political affairs, thus uniting the followers of a tariqa into a quasi political party.

As demonstrated by the Khatmiyya, many tariqas were quasi-governments. In the Khatmiyya, as well as other taruq, there was a hierarchy. Each position in the hierarchy was charged with different responsibilities, making the functioning of the tariqa extremely efficient. Because of this tight organizational control, taruq had the ability to manipulate one against the other. This too was quite reminiscent of the manner in which political parties and interest groups behave. It should not be confused with the tariqa, however, as acting as a "state within a state." The tariqa was the representative of the people. It had considerable ability to voice the concerns of its followers. It was able to put forth the desires of its followers so well that it posed many problems for the legal heads of the regions, and ultimately states.

The Sudanese taruq additionally acted as interest groups as they articulated the needs of their followers to those who were in a position of power. Because they represented enough of the mass society, the tariqas had sufficient power to be listened to. One can say that the tariqa was successful in acting as an interest group or political party since the shaykh, as an elite, was able to maneuver his traditional influence in uniting the tribes and followers under his control into one unified voice. Although the modernization theories asserted during the 1960s proved to be a dismal failure, some of the mechanisms required to prove modernity and development concerning political parties and their actions have legitimacy and can be applied in a limited manner.

Political scientist David Easton put forth the idea that interest articulation and interest aggregation would lead to policy formation, policy execution and policy adjudication. The outputs by the government that are political decisions "constitute a body of specific inducements for the members of a system to support that system."[182] The Sudanese tariqas prove, in this vein, that they were the structures best able to express the desires and needs of their community because of their highly organized and centralized makeup. They then support the system that is in place, as the Khatmiyya did, or revolt against it, as seen with the Mahdiyya. Samuel Huntington asserted societies, which were highly organized, were more capable in articulating the needs and interests of its citizens and achieving their goals.[183] This is further supported by Carl J. Friedrich: "Organized political communities are *better adapted* to reaching decisions and developing policies than unorganized communities."[184] In both the cases of the Khatmiyya and the Mahdiyya, they were able to articulate the interests of their followers as they both had the highly organized structure of the tariqa in place behind them. Because of their ability to express the will of their tariqa, both the Khatmiyya and Mahdiyya were able to influence decisions those in power had to make. In this respect, they both proved to be extremely modern in their approach. Even today, this is similar to actions of lobbyists representing the interests of their groups.

The idea of articulating the will of society does not, however, have its roots in the modernization theories and paradigms advanced during the 1960s or 1970s. In the Islamic religion, the concept of political involvement, whether it be in the form of political parties or interest groups, finds its heritage in the Qur'an. As the Islamic community has its roots in Medina under the Prophet Muhammed, it is not surprising to find that the Qur'an speaks not only of authority, but of how to express the political needs and wishes of the community. The Qur'an states that in order to carry out the business of government, a representative council or assembly should be instituted. This should then be a place where the will of the people can have a voice.[185] The word, which signifies the representative assembly, is *shura*, and the roots of this institution can be found in pre-Islamic societies. The idea of representing the will of the people is considered a very modern and democratic tradition, but it had already existed for centuries within Islam. Additionally, the Qur'an addresses the legitimacy of political parties. In analyzing the passages in the Qur'an, Fazlur Rahman asserts that the Qur'an has prohibited "cliquing," which is sinful and contentious, but political parties are able to exist as long as they do not "degenerate into forces divisive of the community."[186] Because of the tradition of political involvement within the Islamic community, it is understandable why the Sufi tariqa would become a political vehicle. The tariqa could act as a vehicle to challenge the authority in power, such as Muhammed Ahmad did, or to quietly work from within the system to accomplish goals as the Khatmiyya.

The Mahdist Government

The strength of the tariqa in voicing the concerns of the people of the Sudan aided Muhammed Ahmad enormously in gaining support for his Mahdist revolution. With discontent being felt with the perceived injustices from the Turko-Egyptian regime, it was the Sufi leaders, as pointed out in chapter four, who voiced this unrest the best. Muhammed Ahmad exploited this feeling of dissatisfaction by using the Sufist environment. Along with tribal affiliations, taruq were the most important organizational systems in the Sudan at that period. Although each had its own internal structure, Ahmad was able to unite tribal affiliations and taruq together. This not only gave an impression of a religio-political unification to the Turko-Egyptian administration, but more importantly, it gave a sense of solidarity to the Sudanese people.[187] The sense of unity brought on by the coalition of the taruq and tribes came from a sense of holding the same values and mentalities. The connotation of mentalities used here is in the sense of a shared value system and behavior. As the unification effected by Ahmad was one of basically the various Sufi taruq, there was a shared conception of basic Islamic values and behavior. Many people, such as Jean-Yves Calvez, have asserted that holding a shared value system and behavior is actually an obstacle to modernization and development whether it be in the political, societal or economic realms.[188] However, under careful scrutiny, it is exactly these values and behaviors that permitted Ahmad to galvanize the Sudanese Muslims into action. It was this solidarity that initially gave the Mahdist state the strength it needed to be legitimized. Furthermore, the solidarity experienced by the Sudanese was one that gave the Mahdist state longevity, and cohesiveness, even after it ceased to exist. Pierre Bourdieu asserted in an article, "La société traditionnelle" that a group only bands together for a short time to achieve a limited goal. Upon achieving that goal, the unity experienced disintegrates, and the bond no longer exists.[189] By calling on traditional values and behaviors, Muhammed Ahmad was able to unite the Sudanese against the Turko-Egyptian regime. Even after being conquered by the British and Egyptians in 1899, the Sudanese, who believed in his cause, have shown a unity that has continued even until present time.

Part of the basic beliefs that Muslims hold is the belief in a messianic presence, a mahdi, who would bring salvation to the world in general. The Mahdist state was born out of the idea of mahdism. Since Ahmad put forth that he was going to cleanse the Islamic world and offer it salvation, the Sudanese Muslims saw their opportunity to have a place not only in the Sudan, but in the Islamic world as well. The underlying message of ridding the Sudan of the hated foreign administration was the first step in undertaking what was considered at the time, especially in Islamic political philosophy, worldwide salvation. With the support of both the taruq and tribal affiliations, and the threat of being labeled an infidel, this revolutionary message gained enormous legitimacy.

Revolution and violence have also been viewed as impetus to invoke change and modernization. Franz Fanon, political philosopher and former Algerian Ambassador to Ghana, advocated quite strongly that revolutionary methods were important. They were not only necessary to rid a colonized area of an unwanted presence, but moreover, revolutionary methods were the means to creating an independent state, no matter how crude it might initially be:

> Decolonisation is quite simply the replacing of a certain "species" of men with another "species" of men. Without any period of transition, there is a total, complete and absolute substitution. It is true that we could equally stress the rise of a new nation, the setting up of a new State, its diplomatic relations, and its economic and political trends.... The extraordinary importance of this change is that it is willed, called for, demanded.[190]

Fanon went on to uphold that violence was the only way people under foreign domination perceive that they can achieve their independence. Therefore, leaders, such as Muhammed Ahmad, are able to call on those to follow them into an armed resistance. What Fanon points out, quite succinctly, is that violence and revolutions are definitely paths to creating a nation state.[191] In this sense, violence can definitely be considered a path to modernization. The existing foreign regime is ousted and in its place, whether crude or sophisticated, a new independent administration comes into existence. The Mahdist revolution proves Fanon was quite correct in his hypothesis. It is one that has been invoked not only in the Sudan during the nineteenth century, but still is in use in the Islamic world today.

The new state results from the concept of mobilization, or a uniting of human beings into one combined force. It is not only the accretion of humans together, it is that they come together to work in a specific framework. The framework being that they all, whether cognizant of it or not, have a sense of shared ideology.[192] What must occur is a cumulative sense of injustice. This, as according to Meriem Vergès, "encourages disobedience and participation in conflict."[193] It is not one that only is caused by dissatisfaction, but has elements of understanding what is considered unjust and unacceptable. During the Turko-Egyptian administration, the majority of the Sufi taruq had a clear understanding of what they considered both unjust and unacceptable: a foreign rule that opposed their traditional values and behaviors. Mobilization therefore took place in a combined sense of *jihad* (holy war), aimed at ridding the Sudan of the Turko-Egyptian presence, which was in direct conflict with Sudanese Sufi religious beliefs and political aspirations.

In analyzing the path Muhammed Ahmad took in the Sudan, it is obvious that he did create an independent Sudan, albeit under a crude and elementary form of government. There was a three-tiered government, incorporating a supreme command, a financial and a judicial system. Laws were legislated, and moreover, the system set in place was one that was designed to continue even after his death. Muhammed Ahmad not only established an independent state, but he succeeded in uniting the Sudanese people under his rule to make the state work. Unfortunately, because of his policies, there was not a uniform consensus of support. The leaders of the Khatmiyya had to go into exile in Egypt as they did not join in with him, and his later intolerance to Sufi orders put a strain on the state apparatus.[194]

This division would later manifest in the politics seen in the Sudan in present times.

Modern Political Involvement

The Turko-Egyptian administration can be used as the barometer for the beginning of modern political involvement of Sufi orders in the Sudan. Previous to the entrance of the Ottoman Empire into the Sudan, there was little or no involvement of the Sufi orders in political life. With the advent of the Turko-Egyptian joint rule in 1820, political activity rapidly entered the daily life of the taruq. They were recognized as legal entities by the Ottoman rulers and shaykhs. As the heads of the Sufi orders were so influential with their people, the Turko-Egyptian administrators used them to be arbitrators between their followers and the government. Three taruq especially became very influential with the Turko-Egyptian administration: the Khatmiyya, the Idrisiyya and the Majdhubiyya.[195] With this arrival of colonialism, Sufi orders were given more possibilities for expansion. First, colonial governments were not opposed to the expansion of Islam as a whole. It was not seen as threatening. Expansion was used, by many of the neo-Sufis, to overcome many of the animist religions that existed, incorporating them and their believers into tariqas. According to Donal Cruise O'Brien, "the sacred message met a receptive audience with the spreading market economy and the lessening viability of self-isolated subsistence communities."[196] Second, the colonial authorities did not have the infrastructure to disseminate it rules and regulation, nor enforce control. They found it extremely helpful to use Africans as their intermediaries. Those who commanded loyalty explained the law and established a standardized pattern of authority. In many ways, the colonial administrations unwittingly consolidated the power of the Sufi order. Additionally, as pointed out by O'Brien, the colonial governments used the tariqas to help keep peace, collect taxes, and provide military volunteers.[197] This further created the absorption of tariqas into political life. In essence, the tariqa acted as a government, albeit an indirect one, to the existing colonial rule.

Although nonexistent during the Mahdist state, the colonial attitude resurged with the new Anglo-Egyptian administration. When the Mahdist state collapsed, the British desired to incorporate Sudan into their colonial empire. Popular opinion amongst British subjects was that the revolution had taken place as a reaction against the suppressive colonial policies of the Turko-Egyptian administration. As Britain was in the process of expanding their colonial holdings, they desired to annex the Sudan into their control over the Egyptian territory. Additionally, they wanted to assure themselves that France who was also expanding their empire did not get a foothold into Sudanese territory. British involvement in the Sudan stemmed out of the long-term relationship established with the Egyptian *khedive*. It was only through this relationship that Great Britain was justified in entering in the Sudan as they used the pretense of helping Egypt regain its control over the Upper Nile valley. Because of this, Britain was not unable to take complete control, nor was it feasible not to acknowledge Egypt's claims in the region and work out a compromise rule. A combination of the two governments was incorporated in the Anglo-Egyptian Convention of 1899.[198]

Although the Mahdist state had been defeated, that did not mean those who supported Mahdism disappeared nor were inactive. The only element replaced was that of organized resistance. Mahdism as a concept continued to thrive, which gave the new government a sense of insecurity. In the years that followed the end of the Mahdist state, there were several who pretend to be the awaited messianic figure, but they never were able to gather much support from the local people and the fledgling government dealt quite severely with them. This led, however, to the British forming coalitions with those whom they saw as conciliatory towards their foreign rule. It also helped influence the direction of the government's future Islamic policies overall.

At the beginning of the Condominium Era, the joint Egyptian-British rule favored the Khatmiyya, fearing without their support there could be a resurgence of the Mahdist state. The Mirghani family and their followers would become strong allies of the British. Their leader, Sayyid Ali al-Mirghani, was considered to be a stabilizing force for the Sudan and a voice for local opinion. He was an anti-Mahdist, and an alliance with him and his followers assured the Anglo-Egyptian regime of a base of support. This did not mean that the new colonial government desired alliances with Sufi *taruq*. They favored the Khatmiyya because the al-Mirghani family had a long history of loyalty to the Egyptian government and even wished to forge stronger ties. The Khatmiyya was the only tariqa that was accepted under Anglo-Egyptian rule and the rest were regarded with suspicion, thus not recognized officially. The idea of popular Islam of the Sufi taruq was frowned upon. The new administration went so far as to create a Board of Ulema in 1901, which included orthodox officials, the *mufti*, the grand *qadi*, as well as other important prominent people.[199] It was to this Board that the colonial government referred to when decisions had to be made concerning Islam, however, its effectiveness was limited as it has no knowledge of the popular Islam that was prevalent among the indigenous people. The British further encouraged formal orthodox Islam as it encouraged the opening of *khouttabs*, as well as financed construction for building mosques.

The coalition with the Khatmiyya and the push for orthodox Islam remained unchallenged until 1914.[200] At this point a movement know as neo-Mahdism arose, led by Sayyid 'Abd al-Rahman al-Mahdi, the posthumous son of the late Mahdi. He revived the Mahdiyya as a strong national Mahdist organization that would be known hence as the Ansar in the political arena, although his intent was not to enter into the political arena. With the doctrines he put forth, the Ansar transformed itself, interestingly enough into the very entity that the Mahdi originally wanted to abolish: a Sufi tariqa. Sayyid 'Abd al-Rahman al-Mahdi was considered to be quite influential by the Anglo-Egyptian administration, especially as it was perceived that he exerted control over the former revolutionary groups. As there were two major tariqas in the Sudan, the rivalry between them forced the existing regime to placate one or the other, or to align themselves with the order that was felt to be most beneficial at the time. This introduced a new type of *taifiya* or sectarianism into the Sudanese political arena. This new sectarianism was one considered to be associated with economic exploitation of the more rural members of the two groups.[201]

The Khatmiyya and the Mahdiyya both held positions of favor during the Condominium Era, although not at the same time. This had the effect of creating a rivalry between the two tariqas, which one could further liken to that of political parties or interest groups. This rivalry, according to John Voll, was an important element in establishing major Islamic organizations as important political forces.[202] The coalition with the colonial rule illustrates how both parties began to develop and dominate the political scene. The imperial experience gave way to a duality or competition between both tariqas, which furnished the setting for the loyalties of the Sudanese Muslims. This loyalty could be seen quite readily as each faction had its identifying characteristics. For example, during the 1920s, when divisions developed in the Gordon College Old Boys Club, one of the major discernible peculiarities of the division was with which tariqa alliances were.[203]

Both tariqas received the bulk of their support from rural

areas. However, as literacy began to spread in the Sudan, a small but growing educated elite found that they had to be aligned with either the Mahdiyya or the Khatmiyya. Without being connected to either of the two major tariqas, they found they had no political power base. A connection or cooperation was necessary. Religious leaders were also aware society was changing, therefore affiliation with the educated was essential.

In the 1940s, the colliding viewpoints of the Mahdiyya and the Khatmiyya led to the formation of the first legal political parties in which the educated people participated.[204] When political parties formed legally, highly visible religious leaders were courted as they had the ability to bring major religious groups into the political machinery.[205] The Ashigga[206] was the first actual political party in the Sudan. It was formed in 1943 by the late President Isma'il al-Azhari, who was not aligned with the Khatmiyya.[207] A year after it was formed, the Ashigga gained the support of Sayyid 'Ali al-Mirghani as he was annoyed by the political rise of al-Rahman who was a staunch rival and the founder of the Umma party.[208] While Sayyid 'Ali al-Mirghani did not get actively involved in politics, he nonetheless wielded great power from behind the scenes. This party advocated alliance with Egypt as they saw it as the only way to have security from a new Mahdist state arising.[209] The Umma, started in 1945 by Sayyid 'Abd al-Rahman, was supported primarily by those who were supporters of the Ansar, but that did not mean all in the Ansar were part of the Umma party. The Umma became a political party that preferred complete independence and no ties to Egypt.

In 1953, the Ashigga joined forces with other political parties, and emerged as one of the most important factions in the National Unionist Party (NUP). At the same time a third political party emerged on the scene, the Socialist Republicans. This party even though its name suggested a Marxist ideology was actually quite conservative. It was made up of tribal chiefs who agreed with the basic ideology of the Umma, but did not want to be connected with al-Rahman. As it did not gain enough support within the country, the Socialist Republican Party did not last very long. In 1956 and with independence, the NUP split because of a differing of opinions and the Khatmiyya then formed their own political party, known as the People's Democratic Party (PDP).

A key factor to the success of these political parties comes from the already established ideals held by the Sufi tariqas. The Ansar in the Mahdist tradition was able to appeal to those who held strong nationalistic sentiments as the Mahdi had previously laid the foundation of a nationalistic Sudan. Even those not connected to the Mahdist movement, but holding nationalistic views, were able to support the Ansar as it appealed to their personal desire for an independent Sudan. The same mechanism worked for the NUP or Khatmiyya based party. Those who desired a union with Egypt, a pro-unity ideology, were able to align themselves with the Khatmiyya. Even today, the political parties reflect the ideologies of the two major tariqas.

6
Sufi Millenarianism in China

Reform and revitalization were not only nineteenth century African Islamic expressions, manifesting in the Sudan. These ideas and movements have been evident outside the Islamic world where Muslims have not been a majority as well. Muslim minorities have also found that through religion they were able to keep their identify and unite. In China, where the Muslim population has been long-standing and numerous, Sufi brotherhoods proved to be an adhesive element to voice a militant response to the pressures asserted on them to assimilate. Additionally, the Chinese Muslims found their taruq an excellent vehicle to respond to the already existing tension with the Qing dynasty. As in the Sudan, the China taruq prove to hold the ability to be a political force, eliciting responses from within.

The Chinese Muslims are one of Islamic groups scattered throughout the world. There are more Chinese Muslims today than in any Arab country, except for Egypt. Even though in present times, Muslims are spread throughout China, there are two areas with the most dense Muslim populations: the Ningxia region of the Middle Yellow River valley and an expanding area in southwestern Gansu and northeastern Qinghai provinces.[210] Until the creation of the People's Republic of China, most Muslims were generally referred to as *Hui hui* or *Hui jiao* (Hui religion)[211] which comes from the medieval translation for the people of Uigur

(Uygur) (*Huihu, Huihe*), meaning Muslim.[212] They were classified into what was termed a *minzu*.[213] The use of the *minzu* was a way the Chinese classified minority groups. The term Hui came from an attempt by early Chinese officials to classify the Muslim people with whom they had contact. After the formation of the present People's Republic of China, Muslims within its boundaries were classified into ten different *minzu* based on nationality, language and religious background: Hui, Uigur, Kazak. Dongxiang, Kirghiz, Salar, Tadjik, Uzbek, Baoan, Tartar. Those who did not speak a language specific to themselves, such as Chinese or a minority language, such as Tibetan or Mongol (in Sichuan or Yunnan) were classified in the larger category of the Hui.[214] Today, the Hui are the largest group of Chinese Muslims,[215] and are spread throughout the whole country, representing about 8.04% of the nation's population.[216] They are discernible from other Muslims in China as their language is the Chinese regional form, mixed with many Arabic and Persian words, while the other Islamic groups usually speak a Turkic language.[217] Additionally, those of the different groups are designated by ethnonyms: Turkic speakers of the Xunhua region were called Sala Hui, and the Chinese speaking were called Han Hui.[218]

The Chinese Muslims have become Sinicized in many ways. Intermarriage and assimilation have made Chinese Muslims almost indistinguishable from their Han counterparts. From the early days of imperial rule, some have served as governors of provinces, or in lesser administrative positions. They have also been active in the intellectual life of China. By the Ming Dynasty, Chinese Muslims had become very influenced by Han culture. However, it is difficult, according to some scholars such as Jonathan Lipman, Dru Gladney, Joseph Fletcher, to make generalizations about the Hui and other ethnic Muslims, as their practices and adherence to Islam differs from province to province.

It is believed within the Chinese Muslim community that

Islam in China dates back to the beginning of the seventh century when the Caliph 'Uthman sent a representative to the Imperial Court to establish friendly relations with the Tang Emperor Kaotsung.[219] Although there is no proof of an emissary being sent, it is known that Arab and Persian merchants began a lucrative trade with the Chinese very early on, with many establishing a base in cities like Chang'an (Xi'an) and coastal Canton (Guangzhou). Even with laws prohibiting intermarriage with Chinese women, these early merchants, warriors, and traders married Han women, bought land and served in the government. It was through them that the Muslim community grew in China. Over time, the anti-alien laws changed and, for about one thousand years, the Muslim community in some periods enjoyed a special status and peace within the Chinese borders.

The majority of China's Muslims follow the Sunni tradition and the Hanafi School of law, which places them in the mainstream of traditional Islam. The Chinese term for this type of Islam is *gedimu*, a Chinese term for the Arabic *al qadim*, meaning "the ancient."[220] The Sunni tradition is the oldest among China's Muslim population. Before the seventeenth century, the Chinese Muslim associated himself with his mosque. In this way, the Chinese Muslim was no different from his fellow Muslim throughout the Islamic world. In China, however, a distinct difference was discernible between the Muslim and non-Muslim communities. The Muslims were organized within their own self-governed communities, and only associated with their Han counterpart in markets. Their religious organizations were vehicles that created inter-community networks of communication, not only within China, but with the rest of the Islamic world as well. Many of the Chinese Muslims traveled outside China to make pilgrimages to Mecca and to study in other Islamic cites such as Medina.

During the Ming Dynasty, the Muslims community became a permanent part of China as the Chinese leaders in this era were considered enlightened rulers and held an open mind about different religions. Because of this, Islamic missionaries made their way into the country, making the Ming capital city a center for Islamic culture and learning.[221] This tolerance changed dramatically when China came under Manchu rule (Qing dynasty). The transition, although not swift, caused Muslims to be subjected to discrimination and persecution. However, it cannot be said that the Muslim people lived a quiet harmonious life, uninterrupted by persecution before the Qing dynasty. During the Ming dynasty, it has been documented that even though Zhu Yuanzhang, the dynasty's founder, employed Muslims in government positions and the military, there was no attempt to assimilate them into Han ways.[222] A certain amount of anti-Muslim sentiment continued to exist. For the most part, discrimination was not overt, nor did it cause the Muslims to revolt. The Ming period was one in which the Muslims actually established firm and lasting connections with China. However, tensions did accumulate over the centuries.

Starting with the Qing period (1644-1911), Chinese Muslims, especially in the northwest, entered a period of disharmony and unrest. It was a period in which both the Muslim and Han communities exploded.[223] Very early in the Qing dynastic period Sufism entered northwest China from Turkestan. Although, the impact of Sufism was felt in the Muslim world as early as the thirteenth century, it did not have an impression on the Chinese Muslin community until the late seventeenth century.[224] As in the rest of the Islamic world, the movements in China were revolved around the *shaykh* who had founded them. They developed into large socio-economic and religio-political organizations that were referred to in the Chinese language as *menhuan*, meaning the "leading" or "saintly" group.[225] According to the late scholar of Islam and China, Joseph Fletcher:

Over the course of the eighteenth, nineteenth, and early twentieth centuries a considerable number of these "saintly lineages" came into being in northwest China, most of them within the Naqsbandi "path". Typically, each saint's tomb had a shrine, or *qubba* (Chinese *gongbai, gongbei*), and the main shrines became centers for devotional activity. The "saintly lineages" obtained contributions from their followers and amassed substantial amounts of property. The growth in the number and importance of the *menhuan* represented an important change, because they gradually replace the "old" (*gedimu*)[226] pattern by linking together the *menhuan* adherents all over the northwest. The widening compass of social integration that resulted made it easier for the "saintly lineages" and other leaders to harness the Muslims' political and economical potential, facilitating the rise of Muslim warlordism in that region in the twentieth century.[227]

The Naqshbandiyya tariqa was introduced in Gansu to the founder, Ma Laichi, of its first Chinese sub-branch by a Uiguristan Mogul.[228] Founded by Baha' ad-Din Naqshband in the fourteenth century, it was a tariqa that "rejected religious quietism and accelerated their missionary efforts in search of political support, particularly among nomads, whose political strength dominated Central Asia's politics."[229] The main thrust of the Sufi brotherhood was to a distinct stress on Sunni practice, while emphasizing strict adherence to the Sharia. It furthermore was intent on spreading the Islamic religion.[230] It was this objective that led to its spread from Turkestan into northwestern China proper, and the region that is now Tibet.

Towards the end of the nineteenth century, a movement arose from the Sufi brotherhood, the Naqshbandiyya, in the region of Ningxia, stressing Islamic identity, revival of the religion, and militant action against the Qing. The Naqshbandiyya entered China at a very politically charged time. In essence, this was excellent for its consequent spread. Unlike other regions in the Islamic world, the Naqshbandiyya was not confronted with other brotherhoods vying for followers. Instead, Sufism entered northwest China as there was a change in the internal non-Muslim power structure. The Ming dynasty had been overthrown by the Manchu Qing dynasty, which left open hostilities among the Han. One of the first signs of open hostilities erupted one year after the Qing came into power in 1645. Two Muslims were directly involved with the four year revolt that ensued in northwest China, however, they probably did not lead the rebellion because of anti-Muslim sentiments. Their involvement was most likely in connection with basic anti-Qing dispositions and a strong Ming loyalty.[231] Whatever the reasons for Muslims joining into anti-Qing actions, the advent of Sufism gave a means of mobilization and open lines of communication to the disjointed Muslim community. This sense of solidarity had previously been non-existent and afforded the Muslim a chance to strengthen their identity. As the Naqshbandiyya, and consequently its sub-orders, possess a history that has been one of active militant participation in worldly affairs, Muslim political activity was one that could not be avoided. Dru Gladney argues in his book, *Muslim Chinese, Ethnic Nationalism in the People's Republic*, that these orders "advocated more of a "transformationist" perspective, in which they sought to change the social order in accord with their own visions of propriety and morality."[232] The emergence of Muslims, who were previously silent populace in China, caused difficulties with the Chinese authorities who then pursued steps to suppress those involved. Coupled with anti-Muslim sentiment and loyalty to the Ming dynasty, the long accumulated pressure forced the Muslim community to adopt measures and forces of their own, which consequently caused a widening of the gulf between the Chinese and themselves. The pressure, furthermore, brought Muslim identity and culture out of their state of dormancy and compromise.

Ma Laichi introduced a sub-order of the Naqshbandiyya into China that was called the Khufiyya (properly called Khafiyya). The name is taken from the most distinctive feature of the Naqshbandiyya, its silent *dhikr*.[233] Ma Laichi spent many years studying in Yemen and India where the Naqshbandiyya had enormous influence and came back to China intent on reforming the type of Islam that was practiced in his homeland.[234]

One of the first changes Ma Laichi made was instituting the principle of hereditary transmission of *baraka* and in the centrality of *gongbei* in the followers' ritual life.[235] This is very similar to the hereditary transmission that was found in the Khatmiyya within the ranks of the al-Mirghani family. This was known as *menhuan*, or the Muslim saintly family lines found in northwest China.[236] In China, however, Ma Laichi used the existing corporate lineage model that the Chinese had been using for many centuries. It was that incorporated not only *baraka*, but included property holdings, economic activity and active participation in politics.[237] This form, which mixed Sufi tradition and Chinese secular lineages, made the *menhuan* extremely powerful. By the 1750s, because of the social and political standing of these leaders, the Sufis started to have strong tendencies towards political activism. They also vied to gather followers within their own communities as the greater the number of followers, the more prestige a shaykh held. However, the internal fighting that occurred did not always have a positive effect. An example of this in-fighting can be illustrated with the dispute Ma Laichi entered into himself.

According to Joseph Fletcher, Ma Laichi began traveling and preaching with two other Sufis, one being his son, Ma Kuo-pao. As they gathered followers and continued their preaching, an internal dispute arose over how fasting was to be done during Ramadan. Because the Muslim community had no central authority, they decided to take their dispute to the Chinese Imperialist authorities in the region. As there was no way the Qing could resolve the dispute, tensions heightened and became more pronounced. Finally, Ma Laichi was accused of committing heterodoxy, which was in essence committing a crime against the Imperial forces themselves.[238] In many ways, these internal disputes only succeeded in separating the Islamic community, and accentuating the internal problems. As the Qing also were in the process of annexing the Sinkiang region, the disputing only made the large Muslim communities more visible to the Chinese authorities.

Another major response was one of renewing the Islamic culture and revitalizing the Arabic language. Although the Muslim population had been in China for centuries, there were no Islamic texts printed in the Chinese language. To reach as many of the Chinese Muslims as possible, a bi-lingual approach was taken with the Qur'an. This was an unusual step as Muslims believed that the word of the Qur'an is sacred, therefore holding a tendency that it should not be translated. It was only with revivalist movements that a translations began to emerge. This switch occurred because it was felt that it was better not to estrange non-Arabic speaking Muslims, and it would be easier to contain them within the faith. One of the first Islamic texts written in Chinese was done by Wang Daiyu. In an explanation written by Wang, he asserts that the reason he undertook such a laborious task was to enable his fellow Muslim to have accessible a complete guidebook of Islam written in a language they could understand.[239] This bi-lingualism enabled the Chinese Muslims to hold onto their faith and actively participate in the religious ceremonies. The knowledge of Arabic also served as a cohesive measure for the communities, becoming a *lingua franca* used between the different provinces.[240] Arabic, especially its spread during the Qing dynasty, was one of the key elements that spurred revivalism among the Muslims, and then rebellion.

During the eighteenth century, political activism began to gain ground in northwest China. The revivalist movements that were occurring throughout the Islamic world began to penetrate the ideologies of the Sufi orders in China. As mentioned earlier in this work, many Sufi taruq (Qadiriyya, Khalwatiyya, Tijaniyya etc.), were caught up in the change that permeated the Islamic world. The Naqshbandiyya played one of the most pivotal roles in the ensuing revivalist movement. As one of the earliest and most influential centers for the sectarian Sufi movement was Medina, it is not surprising that the Naqshbandiyya would be influential all over the Muslim world. Certainly, as has been demonstrated, its influence penetrated the Sudan in the form of Muhammed Uthman al-Mirghani.[241]

One of the major revivalist movements of that period, the New Sect, came out of Gansu province. It was headed by Ma Mingxin who called for reform of religious practices and a rejection of the compromises that had been made with indigenous Han customs.[242] It was, in essence, a conscious, organized attempt to revive or perpetuate selected aspects on the Islamic culture that seemed to have fallen in dormancy. Raphael Israeli points out in *Muslims in China*:

> Naturally, all cultures seek to perpetuate themselves, and they do this unconsciously as part of the process of individual training and socialization. Conscious and organized efforts to perpetuate a culture can arise only when a society becomes conscious that there are other cultures other than its own, and that the existence of its own culture is threatened by, for example, a process of acculturation to the host culture.[243]

This was exactly what the Chinese Muslims had found they were confronted with. Moreover, the Qing Dynasty had started to decline and many groups were vying for power. The New Sect's ideology had many mystical and spiritual elements in it that seem to have come from Sufi teachings. It is known that Ma Mingxin[244] was associated with the Naqshbandiyya, and it is certain that Sufi thought and ideology were a definite part of his teaching as founder of the New Sect.

As stated earlier, the New Sect, which emerged under Ma Mingxin, had very sectarian and militant overtones. As Ma Mingxin was a member of the Naqshbandiyya, he inevitably brought with him the teaching there should be no deviance from Muslim customs, and furthermore the Muslim should not make any compromise with local Chinese Han customs. As seen with Sufism worldwide, the Chinese Sufis declared their specific beliefs represented a revival or a cleansing. The Chinese Sufi was cleansing his religion of immoral Han ways.[245] This not only caused conflict with the Han, but also caused friction between the Old Sect. The Old Sect, also known as the *gedimu*, held a view that life in this world and the afterlife was inseparable. Therefore, in order to achieve happiness in the afterlife, one had to strive for merit in their life on earth. Because of this, the *gedimu* lived in this real world and not one of mysticism and spirituality. They tended to compromise and assimilate, adopting many of the Chinese customs.[246]

The first signs of Sufi revival can be seen in the disunity, which occurred between the *gedimu* and the *shaykhs* of the Sufi orders. The practice of the *gongbei* tombs being honored by followers of the *shaykhs* was seen as completely unacceptable. The ulema of the Old Sect perceived it as a kind of ancestor worship, thus akin to idol worship. The *gedimu* accommodated the Han, nevertheless, by agreeing to respect and permit their followers to visit those shrines which were in essence non-Muslim. In addition, agreement could not be reached on taxing the Muslim people for repairs to the shrines. This instance was an example of the discord and

Sufi Milenarianism in China   101

different reactions that would remain an identifying factors between the two different Muslim groups that still exist in China today: Sufi Muslims and non-Sufi Muslims (*gedimu*).[247]

Discord also existed between Sufi orders. The most prominent internal conflict among the Sufi orders in China was over the *dhikr*. As pointed out earlier on in this chapter, the Khufiyya followed a silent *dhikr*. This silent method of the *dhikr* has been the most conspicuous feature of the Naqshbandiyya. The Jahriyya followed a vocal one. The two orders entered into many disputes over the correct way to perform the *dhikr*, leading to much bloodshed.[248] There was also fighting over mosque building rights, which territory belonged to whom, over which rituals to follow and to which *shaykh* loyalty would be given. The first signs of Sufi militancy occurred due to internal disputes over Muslim disunity. Around 1780, violence broke out between the Khufiyya and the Jahriyya[249] over an initiation ritual of a New Sufi order and authority of authentic Arabic texts which Ma Laichi, founder of the Khufiyya order, brought back with him when he made a pilgrimage to Yemen.[250] This outbreak of violence was significant as it was characteristic of the disharmony that followed for the next one hundred years between Muslims of different ethnic backgrounds. In addition, it was the start of the extreme militant movements that became prevalent with the New Sect against Chinese authorities. Violence finally climaxed with the Great Rebellion among the northwestern Muslims in 1862.

The Great Rebellion occurred at the time when there was an overall deterioration of direction throughout China. Rebellion had broken out all over China. A major rebellion, the Taiping Rebellion, had been waged and put down. However, smaller ones were still exploding around China.[251] The Muslim rebellion was not an organized revolution against the Chinese state, rather a succession of responses to the persecution various Muslim communities perceived was being waged against them. The Qing authorities had virulently put down the outbreaks of violence between the different Sufi brotherhoods and the punishments meted out were perceived as persecution of the Muslim communities themselves. In addition, there was a widespread fear in the Sino-Manchu regions that the New Sect or the Jahriyya branch would wage open warfare[252] against them.[253] It was acknowledged within the Qing court such a movement would be a inherent danger to the system in place. Sectarian Islam created a sense of awe among the local Chinese as it was a way to cut across different lines of beliefs and unify Muslims from different provinces and districts. Because of this fear, eradication of the New Sect was desired. This was aptly expressed by Zuo Zongtang, the Qing authority in the region:

> If we do not prohibit it, I suspect that in the future they might again rebel.... I have arrested and punished their leaders ... and pasted notices to prohibit it.... When the Xinjiao (New Sect) is extirpated, then Shensi (Shaanxi) and Gansu can be expected to be pacified for many years to come.... Since in other places the preaching of the New Sect is new, future troubles can be adverted if we prohibit it now.[254]

The rebellions that occurred were extremely militant and revivalist in their essence. The most serious of these occurred from 1862 until 1877, and it engulfed the majority of northwestern China, especially Shaanxi and Gansu,[255] including what is known as today as Ningxia.[256] Muslims who felt they had been deprived spiritually had to make a choice between assimilating or try to find a way to generate their own alternative way: rebellion. As the majority of the Muslims at that time were centered in the countryside, and being as economically depressed as the rest of the Chinese in those regions, they chose to align themselves with their own kind instead of any Chinese sectarian movement. In essence, the Chinese Muslims preferred to have their own sectarian movement, as it was the only way they found to pull their disunited ranks together under one unified and official leader. Therefore, they became exceedingly receptive to a message that would take them away from the old ways of what was perceived as institutional Islam. The Jahriyya, as a sub-sect of the Naqshbandiyya, was to deliver the message that seemed sorely needed under the leadership of Ma Hualong.

Ma Hualong, or his followers, who believed he was a direct descendent of the Prophet Mohammed are thought to have promulgated the idea he was the Mahdi, and that he was attempting to establish an Islamic state. As explained earlier, the designation mahdi came to signify a person whose appearance would bring about a lasting age when there would be justice and true belief. Although the concept of the Mahdi has been central to the Shiite beliefs, originally it held no place in Sunni thought. It was only when the first political unrest sprung up that the Sunni followers, in particular those who followed Sufism, began to embrace the concept of a Mahdi. For the Sunni, the notion of the Mahdi is one in which the persona will be a restorer of faith and be chosen for the position rather than making a miraculous return as the Shiite believe. This person will emerge when the world has reached its worst state, restoring the faith and defeating those who are the enemies of Islam.

In China, at the time of Ma Hualong, there was a fertile environment for this type of expectation, particularly when it was coupled with sectarianism. There was not only unrest within the Muslim community as a whole, but there was great unrest among the Han. Militant movements intensified as the Chinese became bent on liberating themselves from Manchu rule. An example of this action was the activity of the White Lotus Society in the 1790s, which had put forth the idea that long anticipated *Maitreya*, or the Buddha of the Future, was coming.[257] This type of popular millenarian Buddhist movement probably induced Ma Hualong to try and put himself forward as the Muslim *Maitreya*, as he feared that the sectarian feelings and ideas of the Muslims would be absorbed by the various Han movements heightening. In essence, he was putting forth the idea of the Mahdi instead of the Han Mandate of Heaven.[258] Both Han and Muslim movements during this period of time had theocratic overtones (the Taiping Rebellion was Christian) and they both basically espoused the same ideals: justice, peace, and abundance. Although the Chinese Han wished to overthrow Manchu rule and establish their own government, this idea was not that of the Muslims. Since Muslims were basically outsiders or foreigners within China, their movement would take on different overtones. It was one of rebellion aimed at breaking with the Chinese and hopefully establishing their own Muslim identity, in addition to attempting to bring the various ethnic groups in the Muslim community together.

This identity was briefly established for a period of eighteen years during which time a Muslim state was in existence. In 1855, a rebellion broke out under the guidance of Du Wenxiu (Tu Wen-hsiu) in the southern province of Yunnan.[259] Du Wenxiu occupied the city of Dali and proclaimed himself Sultan Suleimam of his newly created state. As it was reported that provincial military forces were unable to contain the rebellion, Du Wenxiu was able to control over 360,000 men and 53 cities.[260] As the Qing government was preoccupied with other non-Muslim uprisings, they were not able to retake control of the area until 1873.

It must be mentioned at this juncture that not all Muslims joined in with Ma Hualong or other radical religious leaders. There were many that did side with the government, especially if they adhered to the Old Sect beliefs. These Muslims not only sided with the Qing, but they also fought in their army as well. Many more joined in, though, with the New Sect than did before in earlier rebellions. As pointed out earlier, the most serious of the rebellions date from 1862 to 1877. Most of northwest China was involved in these uprisings. The start of the rebellion occurred with an anti-Qing movement in Shaanxi. In the fight that ensued between the Qing and the rebel troops, many Hui villages were burned. Not only were villages destroyed, there was wholesale murder of both Hui and Han in the capital city of Xian (Shaanxi).[261] The Great Hui Rebellion began right after this incident. Starting in 1862, Ma Hualong focused his activities on Jinjibao.[262] In January of 1871, Ma Hualong was defeated. He was executed on March 2, 1881, [263] along with all of the members of his family.[264] Two years following his death, the Gansu region was put once more under Qing control. As a result of this conflict, the Hui population was radically diminished, to the point of near extinction.[265]

These Muslim uprisings were basically reactions against the Sino-Manchu Imperial administration. They grew out of the need to affirm Muslim identity, especially in the face of the push for assimilation. In many ways the timing at the end of the nineteenth century was favorable for these actions.

The Han were already discontent with Manchu rule. It was unacceptable to them that they were being ruled by people who were lower than they considered themselves. As the Han were letting their discontent known, it presented an opportunity for the Muslims to express their dissatisfaction with the discrimination and persecution that they had been undergoing for a long period of time.

Additionally, the New Sect, being closely associated with the Naqshbandiyya, was exposed to the sectarian movements occurring throughout the Arab world at this time. Sectarian Sufism is usually displayed as a reaction against European imperialism and the inability to stop it. However, in China, Islamic reform and revivalism took the form of a reaction against Qing rule, and assimilation to local Chinese culture. Its roots also came from the deprivation and other socio-political and economic motives plaguing China as a whole. The movement, in the event, was not to dominate and establish a Islamic state, but rather a situation, as classified by Jonathan Lipman as one of "us" versus "them."[266] Its intent was to stop the persecutions from occurring, in addition to taking out retribution on local enemies. In order to justify the response to discontent that Muslims felt at the hands of the Qing, they declared that there should be a revival of their Islamic beliefs and traditions. This was in essence a return to pure Islamic beliefs and ideals, a giving up of their Sinizataion.

Religion cannot be pointed at as the only issue. But it was a vehicle to bind the Muslim community together to protest the policies aimed at them by local control and taxation. Islam acted as a method for the Chinese Muslim to express their overall dissatisfaction with their treatment and the imposition of assimilation being forced upon them. For centuries, Muslims had done everything to hide their culture. They adopted, as Israeli pointed out, "A low profile."[267] Contact with the Chinese world was kept to a minimum, especially when policies were enacted under the Ming to force Muslims into sinicization. Chinese names and language were used, especially in public places. Their domestic lives were outwardly Chinese, but inwardly remained inherently Islamic. In essence, this was a self-effacing method of survival, to live peacefully with the Chinese while safeguarding cultural roots and identities. As long as it was possible to co-exist with the Chinese under relatively tolerable circumstances, Muslims buried their conflicts. However, when there was accretion of anti-Islamic attitudes, the Muslim held the ability to solidify their ranks, calling on their religious beliefs to answer the message they sorely needed.

Ma Hualong was able to emerge as a mahdi figure as it was held that the Mahdi would emerge to end the misery and suffering the people were undergoing. He would

Sufi Milenarianism in China 107

then usher in an era of justice and peace.[268] The setting demanded such a figure. The Chinese had invoked a figure of almost the same religious stature: the *Maitreya* and in recent times they had invoked a Kingdom of Heaven under a "Younger Son of Jesus Christ." Both groups wanted to rid themselves of the Manchu rule. The Chinese wanted to overthrow the government and reestablish their own Han rule, but in many aspects the Muslims were outside of this activity, being detached geographically and spiritually from them. Therefore, the Muslims invoked the Mahdi figure as their Islamic substitute of the *Maitreya* and other Chinese sectarian figures. The Chinese Maitreya could not offer them any type of salvation, but the Islamic Mahdi could. Ma Hualong was accepted as the Muslim *Maitreya* or Mahdi, especially in the northwest, as they sorely needed a figure that could remove them from the misery and discrimination that they were subjected to. Not only did they need someone who could free them from the degeneration of the time, but the fact that he was a Sufi shaykh was of the utmost importance.

As illustrated in chapter five, the Sufi shaykh holds an enormous amount of authority. Although the Chinese tariqa did not have an intact internal organization, the loyalty inspired by Ma Hualong was an important element in the threat that Sufi Muslims posed for the Qing officials. In many ways, he can be compared with Muhammed Ahmad, in that he was able to inspire many Muslims to join in with him in expressing their discontent. Moreover, Ma Hualong not only protected his Muslim community, he was not above protecting those non-Muslims who were under his control.[269] His main appeal was of a charismatic authority, and thus enabling the mobilization his followers. The rebellion waged by Ma Hualong has been alleged by scholars such as Israeli to be a failure since he did not establish a Muslim state.[270] Instead, it should be considered a partial success. Muslim identity emerged from its state of dormancy, uniting a vast community in the northwest. Even if unity did not bring about a Muslim state, the Chinese Muslim created an atmosphere validating future expressions of Islamicism. In this instance, Sufism again showed itself as a factor in political activism.

The underlying question remains to be answered: did the New Sect, being of the Naqshbandiyya order, acquire their ideas of sectarianism from outside of China or did the militant mood prevalent in China help to promote Islamic militancy? It is undeniable that the prevailing conditions of Han sectarianism definitely conditioned the Chinese Muslims to turn to a sectarian movement themselves. They were not immune from the degeneration of the Manchu rule and rebellions exploding around the country. The Taiping Rebellion and the Nian Rebellion were fresh in their minds. Even though these actions on the part of the rebel Chinese were not successful, they had great impact on those who were aware of them. Additionally, the defeat suffered by the Qing administration in the Opium War made many Chinese conscious of the fact that the Qing were not infallible or almighty. As "others" in China, the Muslims demonstrated an anti-Qing sentiment. Therefore, most likely the Chinese Muslim seized the opportunity to rid themselves of the discrimination against themselves.

It cannot, however, be overlooked that Sufi ideas of reviving and reforming the Islamic religion had been spreading for quite a while. All throughout the Islamic world, whether in the Middle East, Africa and Asia, revival and sectarianism had taken hold. The Naqshbandiyya, which embraced these ideals, had already established itself as a militant order in India and certainly had to influence the Chinese branch. The intrinsic belief was to reconstitute Islam in a pure form and revive old practices. This thought predominated most Sufi orders, and produced a unifying effect in China within the Islamic community.

It can be argued that the revival and renewal movement in the Middle East And Africa was and still is today a reaction to European imperialism and westernization. In China, however, European imperialism was not the problem. Rather, it was the overall departure from the Islamic religion to the adaptation of Chinese ways and imperialism from Beijing. The militancy that arose in China was one not to throw off the yoke of a European power, but to cast off the Han ways that had been absorbed by the Muslim population, and forces of expression from the old Chinese empire, now inherited by the Manchu. In essence, this can be compared to casting off a foreign presence. Therefore, a parallelism can be made to similar movements, which were occurring at the same time in the Islamic world. In Africa, the Sudan, a mahdist figure emerged precisely at the same time as Ma Hualong. Although the movement was also to revive Islam, its underlying message was to rid the area of the Turko-Egyptian influence. Another movement similarly would manifest in West Africa in what is the present day country of Nigeria. Thus, the basic nature of Neo-Sufi movements was to rid the Muslim community of a foreign influence. The message, whether in China or other regions, was fundamentally the same: the revival and reform of Islam back to its "Golden Age"[271]. This reflected the prevailing mood of the era.

Today, the Muslim population in China is quite numerous. Although more than eighty percent of the Muslims are non-practicing, they still can be distinguished from their Han counterparts as they follow many of the Islamic customs, i.e. not eating pork. The resistance that was seen in the period of Ma Hualong has revived in the last decade, if not in Gansu and Ningxia, then in Xinjiang.[272] Although the Communist People's Republic has recognized the Muslims as one of the five ancient peoples and permitted them to freely follow their faith, movements have arisen, attesting to the true nature of Islam in calling for strict adherence to its beliefs.

Conclusion

This work has endeavored to prove that modernization is not exclusively a Western phenomenon, occurring only within guidelines established by Western paradigms. Modernization is a process that definitely has the ability to manifest according to Western standards. However, it can result from a variety of expressions. Within Islamic countries, modernization has evolved through changing circumstances over a period of time, especially when aroused by religious expression. Religion, although perceived as a nonmodernizing force, stagnant and seeped in age-old ritual, actually contains a universal language that is understood by its followers. Because of religions' unspoken language of ritual and communal traditions, it actually plays an important role in unifying its followers to accept and execute change as the world modernizes. Sufism has allowed Muslims to respond to the ongoing transition of both societal and political modernity, thus permitting legitimate political parties to arise from brotherhoods in the Sudan, while giving Chinese Muslims a vehicle to oppose existing conditions.

The Khatmiyya demonstrated that Sufi brotherhoods performed an important role by guiding their constituency in a politically active direction. Jean and John Comaroff have pointed out that the Western viewpoint includes an element that "separates rational modernity from the cultures of tradition."[273] However, it was the tradition in Sufi brotherhoods that provided a method of establishing an identity for its followers. The ritual of joining, because one's forebearers did, provided a continuation and a strong identity to a common ground. Sufism, in the Sudan, has shown itself to be a grassroots phenomenon. Those who followed the Khatmiyya identified with the al-Mirghani family. This identification gave the Mirghanis the ability to call upon the tariqa's membership to support a particular idea or goal they wanted to undertake. Even if the objective was that of the Mirghanis, the response of a unified group gave credence to the aspirations or goals. The ability to manipulate was, and remains, all the more stronger because the ritual found in brotherhoods articulates an understood language for the masses.

The promise of achieving entrance into paradise was another method of perpetuating tradition, while at the same time creating a modern network system. The promise was one that gave the tariqa the strength of adherents, thus it created the foundation of a strong network. Networking, whether it be through religious channels or through political channels, ultimately holds the same goal: expression of political intent. In the intricate internal structure of the Khatmiyya, each person had a specific job to do. Each was responsible to report back to a higher person, who ultimately reported to the Mirghanis. In this way, followers held a direct link, through a chain of command, to the shaykh of the tariqa. Communication is a modern guideline of a modern political expression. In order for the wishes of the community to be heard, it must go through a chain of command to a person who is able to express in a viable manner the intent of his followers. As pointed out in this essay, one of the main parameters for modernization is the establishment of interest groups and political parties, which become the technique for involving the masses into the political process. The recognition of political parties stems all the way back to the original community in Medina. Muhammed

Conclusion 113

held an acceptance of political parties, however, they were not intended to represent a division in the community.

Sufi brotherhoods because of their unifying nature hold the ability to speak for a united constituency. Taruq can represent the express desires of the community. Because of this an intrinsic modernizing characteristic is built into Islam, especially through Sufism. These characteristics, whether traceable to the Qur'an or in more recent times, give credence to modernity. Essentially, taruq are means by which political expressions are heard, whether articulated for accommodation or opposition.

The Khatmiyya proved itself to be an excellent example of how a tariqa worked from within to accomplish its goals. It was able to preserve the individual authority of the Mirghani family, while not alienating the Turko-Egyptian regime. The Khatmiyya's basic philosophy of achieving unity with Egypt continued way after that administration lost its power. When the Anglo-Egyptian administration came into power after the Mahdist State, the legitimacy of the Mirghanis was further consolidated. Again, it demonstrated its accommodating nature, thus giving the Anglo-Egyptian regime a way to work with the various communities.

The Mahdiyya following the political tenets originally conceived of by Muhammed Ahmad, can not be viewed a solely a reaction as a resurgence of orthodox religion and Sufism. The reaction at the time was one that reflected the principles of neo-Sufism, stressing activism within society. Independence from a foreign entity brought about a revolutionary spirit within the Sudan, even if the entire country did not agree with Ahmad's ideologies. Although nationalism was not the underscored element within the Mahdist revolution, it did, however, develop as part of the ideology of the modern day party of the Ansar. Even at the present, the Ansar holds strong nationalist ideals while espousing an Islamist government.

Conclusion

One could put forth the argument that the state instituted by Muhammed Ahmad was a theocracy, thus not modern. However, even a theocracy can hold modern elements. The Mahdiyya did voice opposition to the existing Turko-Egyptian administration. It was able to turn the expression of opposition into one of active resistance, thus overthrowing it and establishing an independent country. Whether or not one would classify the rudimentary government as modern, it was one that arose from the mobilization of society, and was fully functional.

Besides having the ability to be networks within a specific area, taruq proved to be the vehicles through which long-range networking was possible. In both the cases of the Sudan and China, the Naqsbandiyya was the means for conveying the neo-Sufist message that was the stimulus for the revivalist movements in both countries. This shared ideology simultaneously gave the Muslim community in the Sudan and China to take the necessary ideology to formulate a response to existing conditions.. In the Sudan, it was a response to a foreign presence in the form of the Turko-Egyptian administration, and in China; the response was against the Qing dynasty. In both countries, mobilization of the Muslim society resulted through Sufi brotherhoods.

Political activism and sectarianism hold the ability to mobilize populations. Whether it be by means of religious expression or not, mobilization is a modernizing force. It creates an atmosphere in which political expressions can be asserted, thus forcing a society to decide the direction they wish to undertake. In itself, this type of expression is modernizing. It forces a careful analysis of the direction of a particular group. In the Sudan and China, the Muslim community had to decide the path they wanted to follow. In both countries, the populous had a choice between accommodation and counteraction. It was these types of choices that forced both societies to undergo the process of determining their political future.

Conclusion 115

Leadership in both countries proved to be extremely effective. If modern leadership must be sensitive and embody the needs and goals of its constituency, then Al-Mirghani, Muhammed Ahmad, and Ma Hualong were perfect case studies. All three were able to communicate to their followers in the symbolic language of the Sufi taruq. They all were able to move their following in a direction of functionality, either expressing their discontent, as in the case of the two former leaders, or reconciliation, as in the case of the latter. As leaders of political activism in their respective countries, al-Mirghani, Muhammed Ahmad and Ma Hualong held the charisma and authority needed to convince their followers to accommodate the changing realities surrounding them.

The political discourse provided by the tariqa was one that created not only leadership, but policy formation, policy articulation and policy determination. The highly structured modus of operandi of the tariqa made these types of decisions feasible. The Sudanese experience was one where the taruq were highly organized, acting as pseudo-governments. This gave them the power to enact a variety of decisions, directly affecting their followers. Although the Chinese experience was not one in which there was a highly structured tariqa, Ma Hualong was also able to promote and elicit a similar response of political activism.

Whereas one can argue religion is not a modernizing force, the real picture is actually much different. Islam, in particular, contains intrinsic political aspects, which Muhammed established from the beginning. This has been verified through both the Qur'an and early writers of Islamic law. Muhammed realized the necessity for political communication, and later intellectuals, such as al-Ghazali, established the necessity to have some type of governance within society. Al-Ghazali successfully showed through his explanation of *siyasa* that religious doctrine can be blended with political ideas, thus demonstrated the legitimacy of political Sufism.

Conclusion

The fact that religion is made use of to communicate to Muslims does not negate modernization from taking place. Modernization does occur by "the dynamic form that the age-old process of innovation has assumed as a result of explosive proliferation of knowledge in recent centuries."[274] The change occurring is multidimensional, taking historical evolution into account. In this respect, modernization results from transformation of a society, not from outright transference of well-defined ideals. By using religion to achieve modernization, Islam provides a place for change, while preserving a cultural framework, which is understood by all. Sufi brotherhoods hold a cultural framework, thus become a modernizing force where they are active.

It must be stressed this endeavor nowhere suggests Islam or Sufism is a modernizing force that achieves democracy and liberalism as advocated by Western modernists. Rather, research proves that different forms of governments, such as those with religious overtones, can be modernizing forces. As in Islam, theological based governments hold the ability to modernize, giving the corresponding societies many different manners of self-expression and response. Sufi brotherhoods, therefore, were, and still are, important associations for expressing political expression.

In Sudanese history, the continued activity of Sufi taruq only supports their involvement in politics. Even though military regimes have come to power in the Sudan since independence, their efforts to exclude Sufi orders from politics has been unsuccessful. In China, Sufism brought about change, especially in the Gansu region. Sufist activity was part of the transformation of empire to nation-state in China, and gave a sorely needed identity to the Sino-Muslim in the midst of upheaval.

One thing cannot be abolished in the Islamic world: Sufi orders cannot be forbidden to exist as religious orders. This has been proven by Mustafa Kemal in Turkey. Even though he forbid the existence of them, not even he was able to abolish the allegiance Sufi orders are were able to command. The allegiance of followers to the religious order assures the support for political activism if called upon. The orders, by virtue of their involvement with the community, therefore, are never apolitical. Because of their religious standing, they have the unique ability to challenge not only other religious leaders, but can challenge a state that gives itself the self-charged right to speak for Islam. Sufi orders provide an internal core along with an identity that Muslim leaders are able to draw and build upon in countries that have a fractured and diverse population, as the Sudan and China. The widespread support of these orders enable them to be an important factor in transforming a radical movement into a fundamental base of conventional politics in many of the modern Islamic societies.

Notes

Introduction

¹ S. H. Nasr, *Traditonal Islam in the Modern World* (London: KPI, 1987) 302-303, and Awad Al-Sid Al-Karsani, "Beyond Sufism: The Case of Millenial Islam in the Sudan" in *Muslim Identity and Social Change in Sub-Saharan Africa,* ed. Louis Brenner (Blomington, IN: Indiana University Press, 1996) 135.

² For the purposes of this work, the Sudan and Sudanese people will refer solely to the Arabicized and Islamicized northern and western part of the Republic of the Sudan. This discussion will not consider the problems of the non-Islamic in the southern part of the country.

³ Caesar E. Farah, *Islam: Beliefs and Observances,* 5th Edition (New York: Barrons, 1990) 296.

⁴ The term "tribe" in Arabic is *qabila*. There are many other different terms in Arabic, which designate further sub-divisions of a tribe, in addition to terms, which mean a larger group of people. As Sudanese scholars regularly use the term "tribe," the word "tribe" and words connected with the term will be used throughout this work. This book does acknowledge the opinion of certain Africanists who believe that the word "tribe" is a creation due to colonization. For detailed information on the creation of tribalism, see: Leroy Vail, *The Creation of Tribalism in Southern Africa,* (Berkeley, CA: University of California Press, 1991).

[5] P. M. Holt, M. W. Daly, *A History of the Sudan, From the Coming of Islam to the Present Day* (Boulder: Westview Press, 1979) 3.

[6] J. S. Trimmingham, *Islam in the Sudan* (London: Oxford University Press, 1949) 81.

[7] During the sixteenth and early seventeenth centuries, the northern Sudan was dominated by two states: the Funj kingdom with its capital at Sinnar, and Darfur in the west. The Funj kingdom was also known as the Sinnar Sultanate because of its capital city, and at some point was converted completely to Islam. The Funj themselves were a dark skinned people whose origins are still obscure. See: Trimmingham, *Islam in the Sudan* and O'Fahey, "Islamic Hegemonies in the Sudan" in *Muslim Identity and Social Change in Sub-Saharan Africa*, ed. Louis Brenner (Bloomington: Indiana University Press, 1993).

Chapter 1

[8] Howard J. Wiarda, "The Ethnocentrism of Social Science," in *Comparative Politics, Notes and Readings*, eds. Roy C. Macridis, Bernard E. Brown, Seventh edition (Belmont, CA: Wadsworth Publishing Co., 1990) 402.

[9] For further treatment on this subject, see: William Shepard, "What is Islamic Fundamentalism," *Studies in Religion/Sciences Religieuses*, January 17, 1988.

[10] Eric Hobsbawm, "Introduction: Inventing Traditons" in *The Invention of Tradition*, eds. Eric Hobsbawm, Terence Ranger (Cambridge: Cambridge University Press, 1983) 1.

[11] Lucien W. Pye, Aspects of Political Development (Boston: Brown, Little & Co., 1965) 8.

[12] E. Vojas. "Problems Connected With Modernization of Underdeveloped Societies" in *Essays in Modernization of Underdeveloped Societies* (Bombay: Thacker and Co., 1971) 493-504.

[13] Dore, R. P. "On the Possibility and Desirability of a Theory of Modernization" in *Report: International Conference on the Problems of Modernization in Asia*, Asia Research Center, Korea University,

Seoul, Korea.

[14] In speaking of the world economy, the definition used here is one put forth by Immanuel Wallerstein in *The Modern World System*, (New York: Academic Press, 1980).

[15] The application of this particular theory has a perfect example in the modernization policies undertaken by Kamal Ataturk in Turkey. In fact, Ataturk's "Six Arrow Plan" is strikingly similar to the theory put forth by Coleman. For further reference on the subject, see: James S. Coleman, *International Encyclopedia of Social Sciences*, 1968 ed., vol. 10, s.v. "Modernization: Political Aspects," 395.

[16] See: Gabriel A. Almond, James S. Coleman, *The Politics of Developing Areas* (Princeton, N.J.: Princeton University Press, 1960).

[17] Samuel P. Huntington, "Political Modernization: America vs. Europe" in *World Politics*, vol. XVIII, April 3, 1966, 378.

[18] As quoted in: Charles Micaud, *Tunisia: The Politics of Modernization* (New York: Preager, 1964) 33.

[19] Richard F. Pfaff, "Disengagement From Traditionalism in Turkey and Iran" in *Western Political Quarterly*, vol. VI, March 1, 1963, 79-98.

[20] See: Hobsbawm, 1-14.

[21] Ibid., 8.

[22] Daniel Crecelius, "The Course of Islam in Modern Egypt," in *Islam and Development: Religion and Sociopolitical Change*, ed. John L. Esposito (Syracuse: Syracuse University Press, 1980) 60., and John L. Esposito, *The Islamic Threat: Myth or Reality* (New York: Oxford University Press, 1992) 10.

[23] Jean Comaroff, John Comaroff, *Modernity and Its Malcontents, Ritual and Power in Postcolonial Africa*, (Chicago: Chicago University Press, 1993) xi.

[24] Ibid., xiv.

[25] Ibid.

[26] Max Weber, *Economy and Society*, eds. Guenther Roth, Claus Wittich (New York: Bedminister Press, 1968) 902.

[27] See: Benedict Anderson, *Imagined Communities*, (London: Verso, 1983).

[28] For further reference, see: Samuel Huntington, *The Clash of Civilizationsand the Remaking of the New World Order* (New York: Touchtone, 1996).

[29] Ibid., 96.

[30] See: David E. Apter, *Rethinking Development Modernization, Dependency and Postmodern Politics* (Beverly Hills, CA: Sage Publications, 1987).

Chapter 2

[31] For further discussion and description of the Twelvers and Ismailis, see: John Esposito, *Islam the Straight Path*, 45-48.

[32] This is an extremely broad definition, which probably will not please everyone who reads this explanation. However, it is virtually impossible to categorize all the different beliefs and reasons that one adheres to the Sufi practice.

[33] J. Spencer Trimingham, *The Sufi Orders in Islam*. (Oxford: Clarendon Press, 1971) 1.

[34] "The Principle of Following the *Sunna*" in *Book XX of Al-Ghazali's Ihya' 'Ulum al-Din*.(The Revitalization of the Sciences of Religion) trans. L. Zolondek. (Leiden: E. J. Brill, 1963) 7.

[35] John O. Voll, "Sufi Thought and Practice" in *The Oxford Encyclopedia of the Modern Islamic World*, ed. John L. Esposito (NewYork: Oxford University Press, 1991) 102.

[36] For a concise description of the Ummyad caliphate and its achievements, see: Philip K. Hitti, *A History of the Arabs*, 10th edition (New York: St. Martin's Press, 1970).

[37] For further treatment on the subject, see: Arthur J. Arberry, "Mysticism" in *The Cambridge History of Islam*, ed. Peter M. Holt, Ann K. S. Lambton, and Bernard Lewis, (Cambridge: 1970) vol. 2. 604ff., esp. 605.

[38] L. P. Elwell-Sutton, "Sufism and Pseudo-Sufism" in *Islam in the Modern* World (New York: St. Martin's Press, 1983) 50.

[39] Bassam Tibi, *The Crisis of Modern Islam, A Preindustrial*

in the Scientific-Technological Age, (Salt Lake City: University of Utah Press, 1988) 69.

[40] His most famous work is *The Revival of Sciences.* It is not, however, the intention of this author to delve deeply into the theology or doctrine of al-Ghazali. For a further reference, see: W. Montgomery Watt, *Muslim Intellectual: A Study of Al-Ghazali* (Edinburgh: The Edinburgh University Press, 1963) and Fauzi M. Najjar, "*Siyasa* in Islamic Political Philosophy" in *Islamic Theology and Philosophy: Studies in Honor of George F. Hourani.* (Albany: State University of New York Press, 1984).

[41] "The Principle of Following the *Sunna*" in *Book XX of Al-Ghazali's Ihya' 'Ulum al-Din.* (The Revitalization of the Sciences of Religion) 11.

[42] Referring to governance, politics, administration. See: *A Learners Arabic-English Dictionary,* ed. F. Steingass (New Delhi: Gaurav Publishing House, 1994) 520.

[43] For further reference on the subject of *siyasa,* see: Najjar, 92-93.

[44] Albert Hourani, *Arabic Thought in the Liberal Age 1798-1939,* (Cambridge: Cambridge University Press, 1983) 13-15.

[45] John O. Voll, *Islam, Continuity and Change in the Modern World,* (Syracuse: Syracuse University Press, 1983) 12.

[46] J. S. Trimingham, *Sufi Orders in Islam,* 4.

[47] This word is a Sudanese derivative from the classical Arabic *faqih* which means "jurist," or a learned and holy man, and also implies being a poor Sufi teacher. The singular, *faqie,* means a poor person, possibly even a peasant.

[48] B.G. Martin, *Muslim Brotherhoods in Nineteenth Century Africa* (Cambridge: Cambridge University Press, 1976) 2.

[49] As this chapter will be speaking mostly about the Sudan, it is necessary to point out that this stage of development did not occur in the Sudan. As is stated by Ali Salih Karrar, there were only two developmental stages in the Sudan: pre-tariqa and tariqa. For further reference, see: Ali Salih Karrar, *Sufi Brotherhoods in the Sudan.* (Evanston, IL: Northwestern University Press, 1992).

[50] Trimingham, *Sufi Orders in Islam,* 9.

[51] John O. Voll, *Islam, Change and Continuity in the Modern*

World, 13.

⁵² The term "Mirghaniyya" is sometimes incorrectly used to identify the tariqa lead by the Mirghani family. The Mirghaniyya is a set of devotional exercises and litanies put together by a grandfather of Muhammed 'Uthman, and then incorporated by him into the Khatmiyya. Another definiton given to the origin of the word by J. S. Trimmingham is the township in which the Khatmiyya orginated. For further refernce on that definition, see: J. S. Trimmingham, *The Sufi Orders in Islam*, 117.

⁵³ Ibid., 10.

⁵⁴ Neo-Sufism has caused some controversy within the academic world. Not all scholars, for example: O'Fahey, find the term neo-Sufism acceptable as they feel it ignores important continuities in Sufi tradition. Furthermore, some scholars say the term tends to lend a belief there are much more similarities between different tariqas than there actually are. However, the evolution of Sufism has produced a new use of tariqas in many instances such as political vehicles. In the case of this study, the term neo-Sufism, if used, will apply to those taruq that engaged in political activity. Therefore, the word, neo-Sufism, for this work seems not only correct, but appropriate as well. For further treatment of "neo-Sufism" in depth, see: Fazlur Rahman, *Islam*. (New York: Anchor Books, 1968), chapter 12, and Nehemiahh Levtzion, John O. Voll, *Eighteenth Century Renewal and Reform in Islam*. (Syracuse: Syracuse University Press, 1987). For the controversey over this term and the inherent changes in eighteenth century taruq, see: Nehemiah Levtzion, "Eighteenth Century Sufi Brotherhoods, Structural, Organizational and Ritual Changes" in *Islam: Essays on Scripture, Thought and Society, A Festschrift in Honour of Anthony H. Johns*, ed. Peter G. Riddell, Tony Street (Leiden: Brill, 1997) 147-148.

⁵⁵ Levtzion & Voll, 10.

⁵⁶ The *Hadith* is a statement or account of a saying or action of the Prophet. These accounts are were collected during the Middle Ages, and furnish an authoritative basis for Islamic law, complementing the Koran.

[57] For further treatment on the subject, see: John O. Voll, *Islam, Change and Continuity in the Modern World.*

Chapter 3

[58] This dualism and parallelism found during the eighteenth and nineteenth centuries has ended in varying degrees, depending on the transformation of the culture found in a particular region. For further reference, see: Abdullahi Ahmed An-Na'im, "Islam and Human Rights in Sahelian Africa" in *African Islam and Islam in Africa: Encounters between Sufis and Islamists.* Ed. Eva Evers Rosander, David Westerlund (Athens, Ohio: Ohio University Press, 1977) 80.

[59] Al-Karsani, Awad Al-Sid, "Beyond Sufism: The Case of Millennial Islam in the Sudan" in *Muslim Identity and Social Change in Sub-Saharan Africa*, ed. Louis Brenner (Indianapolis: Indiana University Press, 1993) 136.

[60] For further reference, see: M. Delafosse, "L'Animisime nègre et sa resistence a l'Islamisation en Afrique occidentale," *R. M. M.*, Mar 1992, vol. XLIX, 121-164

[61] The Funj themselves were a dark skinned people whose origins are still obscure. See: Trimmingham, *Islam in the Sudan* and O'Fahey, "Islamic Hegemonies in the Sudan" in *Muslim Identity and Social Change in Sub-Saharan Africa*, ed. Louis Brenner (Bloomington: Indiana University Press, 1993)

[62] P.M. Holt, *Studies in the History of the Near East*, (London: Frank Cass, 1973) 122.

[63] Ibid., 121.

[64] Ibid..

[65] P.M. Holt, *A Modern History of the Sudan*, (New York: Grove Press, Inc., 1961) 31.

[66] Ibid., 30.

[67] Karrar, 20.

[68] P. M. Holt, M. W. Daly, *A History of the Sudan*, 32.

[69] See: J. S. Trimmingham, *Islam in the Sudan*, 42-43, note 3.

[70] Voll, *Islam, Continuity and Change in the Modern* World, 77.
[71] Karrar, 35.
[72] Ibid., 36.
[73] Voll, *Islam, Change and Continuity in the Modern World*, 21.
[74] Richard Olaniyan, "Islamic Penetration of Africa" in *African History and Culture*, ed. Richard Olaniyan (Lagos, Nigeria: Longman Nigeria Ltd. 1982) 42.
[75] For further reference on this subject, see: Albert Hourani, *Arabic Thought in the Liberal Age 1798-1939* (London: Cambridge University Press, 1967).
[76] Karrar, 42.
[77] There are four major schools of Islamic jurisprudence: *Maliki, Hanafi, Hanbali*, and *Shafi*. Each school is more prevalent in different parts of the Islamic world. *Maliki* is the prevailing legal school in sub-Saharan Africa.
[78] Voll, *Islam, Continuity and Change in the Modern World*, 77.
[79] Trimmingham, *Islam in the Sudan*, 110.
[80] For further treatment on the subject, see: Voll, *Islam Continuity and Change in the Modern World*, 102-103.
[81] Voll. *Islam, Change and Continuity in the Modern World*, 77.
[82] A joint Turko-Egyptian rule began in the Sudan in 1820 and lasted until the 1885. It is called Turko-Egyptian as Egypt was still part of the Ottoman Empire at the time. The rule has been categorized as Turko-Egyptian as the main administration was Egyptian. Although, there were British appointed officials, such as Charles Gordon who became the governor-general before the regime was about to collapse under the Mahdi's jihad. This chapter, however, will not deal with the history of this rule. For further information, see: P. M. Holt, *A History of the Sudan*.
[83] For treatment of the slave trade in the southern Sudan, see: Carolyn Fluehr-Lobban, "Islam in the Sudan A Critical Study" in *Sudan, State and Society in Crisis*, ed. John O. Voll (Bloomington: Indiana University Press,) and Richard Olaniyan, *African History and Culture*, (Lagos, Nigeria: Longman Nigeria Ltd. 1982) 45-52, 61-71.
[84] The emergence of the Sammaniyya in the Sudan by Ahmad

al-Tayyib has been given different dates by different scholars. For example, see: Holt, *A History of the Modern* Sudan, 32, and Karrar, 43,

[85] For further reference, see: Karrar 47-48, and Trimmingham, *Islam in the Sudan,* 126.

[86] Nicole Grandin, "Les taruq au Soudan dans la Corne de l'Afrique et en Afrique orientale" in *Les Ordres Mystiques Dans l'Islam Cheminements et situation actuelle,* ed. A. Popovic, G. Veinstein (Paris: Editions de l'Ecole des Hautes Etudes en Sciences Sociales, 1983) 174.

[87] Karrar, 54.

[88] For further reference on the subject, see: Karrar, 62-64.

[89] Shaqiyya is the term used to describe the most important ethnic group of the northern reverain region. According to R. S. O'Fahey and J. L. Spaulding, this term does not come into existence before the arrival of the Arabs from the fourteenth century onward. For further reference, see: R. S. O'Fahey, J. L. Spaulding, *Kingdoms of the Sudan* (London: Metheun, 1974).

[90] Dervishes (*taqashshuf*) were those Sufis who when they abandoned themselves to their *dikr,* end up whirling around in a dizzying circle, hence the name whirling dervishes.

[91] Karrar, 68-70.

[92] For further general reference, see: J. S. Trimmingham, *Islam in the Sudan,* 235-236.

[93] John Voll, "A History of the Khatmiyya Tariqah in the Sudan", Ph.D. thesis, Harvard University, 1969, 153.

[94] The *shaykh al-sajjada* was called the master of the prayer rug or skin because it was inherited from the founder of the order. Trimmingham, *Islam in the Sudan,* 173.

[95] Unless otherwise noted, the following information on the organizational structure is based mainly of Karrar's *The Sufi Brotherhoods in the Sudan* as there is not an abundance of material on the subject.

[96] "*Al-Sayyid*" is the most common term attributed Al-Mirghani, and it emphasizes the claim of descent from the Prophet Muhammed.

[97] Ahmad Al-Shahi, "Sufism in Modern Sudan" in *Islam in the*

Modern World, ed. Denis MacEoin, Ahmad Al-Shahi (New York: St. Martin's Press, 1983) 63.

[98] For the position and responsibilities in other taruq, see: Trimmingham, *Islam in the Sudan*, 175.

[99] Ibid.

[100] For further reference, see: Trimmingham, *Islam in the Sudan*, 174-175.

[101] Karrar, 131.

[102] See: Trimmingham, *Islam in the Sudan*, 175, Karrar, 133.

[103] Ibid., 175, n2.

[104] Karrar, 133.

[105] It is not the intention of this author to go into the rules of behavior within the Khatmiyya, or as it would also pertain, to other Sufi orders. The purpose here is to point out that rules and regulations did exist, which did control a good part of all adherents lives. For further reference on the subject, see: Karrar, 133-164, and Trimmingham, *Islam in the Sudan*, 176-216.

[106] Muhammed 'Uthman al-Mirghani accepted totally the existence of the Isma'iliyya because it originally was a branch of the Khatmiyya. Al-Mirghani authorized his student, Isma'il ibn Abdallah al-Kordofani, to found his own tariqa around 1813. For further reference, see: Grandin, 181-182, ff66, 198.

[107] Even though the followers of the Khatmiyya were forbidden entrance into another tariqa, this did not preclude a member of the Mirghani family from having other associations. Al-Mirghani himself was a member of different taruq, such as the Naqshbandiyya and Sammaniyya, although he had joined them before creating his own tariqa.

[108] J. S. Trimmingham, *The Sufi Orders in Islam*, 118.

[109] It must be pointed out at this juncture not all scholars attribute this particular event and the relation with the Shayqiyya as a factor in the consolidation and spread of the Khatmiyya. Voll, al-Shahi, among others, lean in this direction; for example, see: Voll, thesis (1969), Al-Shahi, "A Noah's Ark: the Continuity of the Khatmiyya Order in the northern Sudan", *Bulletin, British Society for Middle Eastern Studies*, viii/1, 1981, 16. Karrar points out that

the Turko-Egyptian regime favored other taruq as well, and that the majority of the followers from the Shayqiyya region were not of the ethnic group themselves.

[110] Al-Shahi, 63.
[111] Voll, *Islam, Change and Continuity in the Modern World*, 141.
[112] Al-Shahi, "Sufism in Modern Sudan," 63.
[113] P.M. Holt, *The Mahdist State in the Sudan 1881-1898 a Study of Its Origins Development and Overthrow*, 2nd Edition, (Oxford: Clarendon, 1970) 32.
[114] Alexander S. Cudsi, "Islam and Politics in the Sudan", *Islam in the Political Process*, James P. Piscatori, ed. (Cambridge: Cambridge University Press, 19) 37.
[115] Carolyn Fleuhr-Lobban, "Islamization in the Sudan, A Critical Assessment," 76.
[116] P.M. Holt, *Studies in the History of the Near East*, 126.
[117] The financial problems of Egypt, with its finances mortgages to European bankers, were so severe that the British took over the government in 1882 after a failed nationalist uprising.

Chapter 4

[118] It is not the purpose of this chapter to give more than an general overview of the beginning of the Mahdiyya and its organization. The chapter's intent is to be a prerequisite for an analysis of how it became a major political party.
[119] P.M. Holt, *A Modern History of the Sudan*, 77.
[120] Ibid..
[121] For further reference, see: Gabriel Warburg, *Historical Discord in the Nile Valley* (Evanston, IL.: Northwestern University Press, 1992) and Muhammed Mahmoud, "Sufism and Islamism in the Sudan" in *African Islam and Islam in Africa, Encounters between Sufis and Islamists*, David Westerlund, ed. Eva Evers Rosander (Athens, OH.: Ohio University Press, 1997).
[122] Mahmoud, 172.
[123] The singular in Arabic is *alim*.

[124] Voll, *The Sudan, Unity and Diversity in a Multicultural State*, 40.

[125] If one looks carefully at the makeup of the different Sufi orders, it becomes obvious there is an affinity of tribal groups belonging to a particular tariqa. The different regions had various tribal coalitions and they tended all to belong to the same tariqa.

[126] For further reference to this topic, see: P.M. Holt, *Studies in the History of the Near East*. ch. 7.

[127] The name Khatmiyya clearly indicts that al-Mirghani believed that he had received a divine revelation.

[128] P.M. Holt, R. W. Daly, *The History of the Sudan, From the Coming of Islam to the Present* (Boulder, CO, 1963) 88-89.

[129] Starting in 1822, after the Egyptian administration took over the control of education, many Sudanese were educated at al-Ahzar University in Cairo. This training further eroded the authority the local *fakis* held. Fleuhr-Lobban, 74.

[130] Holt, *Studies in the History of the Near East*, 142.,

[131] In August 1877, the Khedive Is'mail of Egypt and the British government held a convention: the Slave Trade convention. This put a stop to the trade of the Negroid population and Abyssinians throughout all Egyptian territory, prohibiting the purchase and sale of slaves in the Sudan by 1889. For concise reference on the treatment of ending the slave trade in the Sudan, and the conquest of Khartoum, see: P. M. Holt, *The Mahdist State in the Sudan 1881-1898* (Oxford: Clarendon Press, 1970).

[132] The Baqqara tribes were located in the northern part of the Sudan, along the second and third cateract of the Nile that runs across the Nubuan Desert.

[133] Gabriel Warburg, *Islam, Nationalism and Communism in a Traditional Society: the Case of the Sudan*, (London: Frank Cass and Co., 1978) 12.

[134] Warburg,, *Historical Discord in the Nile Valley*, 11.

[135] Grandin, "Les Taruq au Soudan," 174, 196 ff42.

[136] Ibid.

[137] Antonio Palmisano, *Ethnicity: the Beja as Representation. Ethnizitat and Gesellschaft*. Occasional Paper 29, (Berlin: Das Arabische Buch, 1991) 17.

[138] The first modern entity is considered to be Muhammed Ali's Egypt. In the Sudan, Islamic nationalists assert that this was the beginning of the real process of national unification, opposed to being simply a more centralized system of political authority.

[139] The second quote according to P.M. Holt is taken from Naum Soucair, *Ta'rikk al-Suda al-qadim wa-l-hadith wa-jughrafiyatuh*, Cairo 1903, and is a later version. It is much closer to the original spoken between Muhammed and his followers. Holt, *The Mahdist State in the Sudan*. 117 & 117, n2.

[140] Ibid.

[141] It is necessary to clarify the meaning of the term as used here since it has been used before in speaking of the organizational structure. In the Khatmiyya, the title was used to designate a certain position within the tariqa. In the Sudan, the title has become one that is accepted to mean one who is a deputy of a religious order, or the local representative. In Islam, the term means one who is successor to the Prophet Muhammed as was illustrated by the title given to Abu Bakr: *Khalifa al-Saddiq*.

[142] The Mahdi offered the title of *khalifa* to four of his chosen people. All but one, "Successor of Uthman," was left vacant because the person he chose, Muhammad al-Mahdi b. al-Sanusi, rejected the offer.

[143] Warburg, *Islam, Nationalism and Communism*, 13.

[144] They were the ones most directly involved with the slave trade and affected by the outlawing of slavery under Gordon.

[145] This is known as the *hijra* to Qadir. The Mahdi urged hijra, which is the flight for the faith from the infidel to the Mahdi. This is one of the earliest examples of the Mahdi's conscious parallel to the life of Muhammed; Muhammed made a hijra to Medina from Mecca. This particular *hijra* brought about the loyalty of the Baqqara tribes, thus increasing the amount of followers who joined in with the Mahdi.

[146] Holt, *The Mahdist State...*, 125.

[147] Ibid., 121.

[148] Holt, *The History of the Sudan*, 125-127.

[149] Holt, *The Madhist State*, 128.

Chapter 5

[150] Peter Woodward, "Sudan: Islamic Radicals in Power" in *Political Islam Revolution, Radicalism or Reform?* John L. Esposito, ed. (London: Lynne Rienner Publishers, 1997) 95.

[151] In this chapter, the Mahdiyya will be referred to as a tariqa. It is not incorrect to refer to it as such at this point in this analysis because Muhammed Ahmad's posthumous son, Abd al-Rahman, will ironically turn the movement into a "tariqa-style" organization between 1914-1924.

[152] Al-Shahi "Sufism in Modern Sudan," 58.

[153] Bernard Lewis, *The Political Language of Islam* (Chicago: The University of Chicago Press, 1988) 94.

[154] The Anglo-Egyptian Condominium started in 1899 with the conquest of the Mahdist state. The British asserted their sovereignty based on the fact they actually conquered the Sudan, while Egypt based their right to have a joint rule because they were locked in disputes with certain provinces. Both flags flew over the country as per agreement. For further reference on the Anglo-Condominium era, see: P.M. Holt, D. W. Daly, *The History of the Sudan*.

[155] Ibid., 148.

[156] Voll, *Change and Continuity in the Modern World*, 5.

[157] John L. Esposito, *The Islamic Threat Myth or Reality* (New York: Oxford University Press, 1992) 14.

[158] See: chapter 3, page 38.

[159] Holt, *The History of the Sudan*, 59.

[160] For further treatment on the subject of "sacred authority," see: Eickelman & Piscatori, *Muslim Politics* (Princeton: Princeton University Press, 1996) 46-79.

[161] According to 1996 statistics, the literacy rate in the Sudan was only 32%. Some have argued this figure putting the literacy rate at only 3%. However, it can safely be stated that in the nineteenth and early twentieth centuries, the literacy rate was very low. For further reference, see: A. A.Raziq & M. A. Bushra, "Democratic Republic of the Sudan" in *The International Handbook off Higher*

Education (San Francisco: Jossey-Bass, 1977) pp. 4005-4010.

¹⁶² Nehemiahh Levtzion, "Eighteenth Century Sufi Brotherhoods" in *Islam: Essays on Scripture, Thought and Society. A Festschrift in Honour of Anthony H. Johns* (Leiden: Brill, 1997) 151.

¹⁶³ Hannah Arendt, "Communicative Power" in *Power,* Stephen Lukes, ed. (Oxford: Blackwell, 1986) 59-74.

¹⁶⁴ Eickelman & Piscatori, 58.

¹⁶⁵ For further reference, see: Max Weber, *Max Weber on Law in Economy and Society (Wirtshaft und Gesellschaft)*, 20th Century Legal Philosophy Series, ed. Max Rheinstein. Trans. Edward Shils and Max Rheinstein, vol. VI. (Cambridge, MA: Harvard University Press, 1954) 336.

¹⁶⁶ Frederick Mathewson Denny, *An Introduction to Islam* (New York: Macmillan Publishing Co., 1994) 246.

¹⁶⁷ Ibid., 246-247.

¹⁶⁸ *Qur'an*, 49: 13.

¹⁶⁹ Sayyid Jamal al-Din al-Afghani, "Islamic Solidarity" in *Islam in Transition*, John L. Donahue, John L. Esposito, eds. (New York: Oxford University Press, 1982) 21-22.

¹⁷⁰ For further reference see: Lewis, *The Political Language of Islam*, 68-70.

¹⁷¹ For further reference, see: Lucien W. Pye, *Aspects of Political Development* (Boston: Little, Brown & Co., 1966) 108-110.

¹⁷² Voll, "Sufi Thought and Practice" 108.

¹⁷³ For further treatment on this subject, see: Eickelman and Piscatori, *Muslim Politics*, 46-74.

¹⁷⁴ Al-Afghani, 22.

¹⁷⁵ Weber, 337.

¹⁷⁶ See: Donal B. Cruise O'Brien, Christian Coulon, *Charisma and Brotherhood in African Islam* (Oxford: Clarendon Press, 1988) 2-7.

¹⁷⁷ *Baraka* is not always inherited. For example, in the case of Sufi taruq, a founder does not usually inherit *baraka*; it is bestowed by Allah.

¹⁷⁸ François Constantin, "Charisma and Power in East Africa" in *Charisma and Brotherhood in African Islam*, eds. Donal Cruise O'Brien, Christian Coulon (Oxford: Clarendon Press, 1988) 87-88.

[179] During the nineteenth century, the headquarters of the Khatmiyya in the Sudan was actually in the Khatmiyya village in Kassala. It was only in the twentieth century that the administration center was moved to Khartoum.

[180] R. G. Jenkins, "The Evolution of Religious Brotherhoods in North and Northwest Africa 1523-1900" in *Studies in West African Islamic History*, 59.

[181] For further reference on the functions of political parties, see: Manfred Halpern, "Political Parties" in *The Developing Nations What Path to Modernization?* ed. Frank Tachau (New York: Dodd, Meade & Co., 1974) 119.

[182] For a complete analysis of structure-functionalism, see: David Easton, "An Approach to the Analysis of Political Systems" in *World Politics* 9, no. 3 (Princeton: Princeton University Press, 1957) 383-400.

[183] Samuel Huntington, "Political Development and Decay" in *Political Modernization* , ed. Claude E. Welch Jr. (Belmont, CA: Wadsworth Publishing Co., 1967) 229-330.

[184] Carl J. Friedrich, *Man and His Government* (New York, 1963) 150. (Italics are in original)

[185] *Qur'an*: 42:38.

[186] Ibid., 44.

[187] Mahmoud, 177.

[188] For further treatment of this subject, see: Jean-Yves Calvez, *Aspects Politique et Sociaux des Pays de Developpment* (Paris: Dalloz, 1971), chapter 11.

[189] Pierre Broudieu, "La société traditonnelle," *Revue de sociologie du travail* (January-March, 1963) 24-43.

[190] Franz Fanon, "Violence Will be the Midwife of the New World" in *The Developing Nations What Path to Modernization?* ed. Frank Tachau (New York: Dodd, Mead & Co., 1974) 187.

[191] Ibid., 187-197.

[192] Merien Vergès, "Genesis of a Mobilization: The Young Activists of Algeria's Islamic Salvation Front" in *Political Islam Essays from Middle East Report*, eds. Joel Beinin, Joe Stork (Los Angeles, CA: University of California Press, 1997) 299-301.

[193] Ibid., 300.
[194] See: chapter 4, 9-10.
[195] Mark Huband, *Warriors of the Prophet The Struggle for Islam* (Boulder, CO.: Westview Press, 1998) 142.
[196] Donal Cruise O'Brien, "Islam and Power in Black Africa" in *Islam and Power*, eds. Alexander C. Cudsi and Ali E. H. Dessouki (Baltimore, MD: Johns Hopkins University Press, 1981) 161.

An example, cited by O'Brien, is a small trading Muslim minority in Tanganyika, which grew from a fraction at the time of German occupation to a 40% Muslim population by independence. Of the Muslim total, 70 per cent were associated with the Qadiriyya order.

[197] Ibid., 162.
[198] P.M. Holt, MW Daly, *A History of the Sudan*, 102.
[199] Ibid., 107.
[200] Mahmoud, 179.
[201] Ibid.
[202] Voll, *The Sudan: Unity and Diversity in a Multicultural State*, 53.
[203] John Voll, "Mahdis, Walis, New Men in the Sudan" in *Scholars, Saints, and Sufis Muslim Religious Institutions Since 1500*, Nikki R. Keddie, ed. (Berkeley: University of California Press, 1972) 374.
[204] Al-Shadi, "Sufism in Modern Sudan," 64.
[205] Voll, "Mahdis, Walis, New Men in the Sudan," 375.
[206] Ashigga is an Arabic word '*ashiqqa*,' meaning brothers of the same mother and father.
[207] Al-Shahi, "Sufism in Modern Sudan," 64.
[208] P. M. Holt, M. W. Daly, *The History of the Sudan*, 148.
[209] Ibid.

Chapter 6

[210] The first region is now known as the Ningxia Hui Autonomous Region. Jonathan N. Lipman, *Familiar Strangers A History of Muslims in Northwest China* (Seattle: University of Washington Press, 1997) 3.

[211] The Muslims in China are still referred to as Hui, unless they are designated by the particular ethnic group. From this point on as it is an accepted term, it will not be italicized.

[212] Dru C. Gladney, *Muslim Chinese Ethnic Nationalism in the People's Republic*. Harvard East Asian Monographs 149 (Cambridge, Mass: Council on East Asian Studies, Harvard University, 1991) distributed by Harvard University Press. 18.

[213] According to Jonathan N. Lipman, there is no English translation for this word. It was formally known as *shaoshu minzu*, although shortened to just *minzu*. The use of this term dates back to the Tang and Yuan dynasties, but there is no mention of it during the Ming. It does not come back into use until the formation of the People's Republic of China. For further reference, see: Jonathan N. Lipman, *Familiar Strangers*, xx-xxv.

[214] Gladney, 19-20.

[215] Most of the Hui are non-practicing Muslims. They are discernible because they do not eat pork, which is forbidden by the Islamic religion.

[216] Gladney, 27.

[217] Michael Dillon, *China's Muslims* (Hong Kong: Oxford University Press, 1996) 6.

[218] Lipman, *Familiar Strangers*, xxiii.

[219] Caesar E. Farah, *Islam*, (.New York: Barrons, 1994) 278.

[220] As will be explained further on, this term will also be the name used for the Old Sect who are usually not members of the Sufi orders. See: Michael Dillon, *China's Muslims*. (Hong Kong: Oxford University Press, 1996) 19-20.

[221] Ibid., 17-18.

[222] Lipman, *Familiar Strangers*, 39.

[223] Raphael Israeli, *Muslims in China, A Study in Cultural Confrontation*. (London: Curzon Press, 1980) 129-131.

[224] Gladney, 41.

[225] Ibid.

[226] The *gedimu* were the first Islamic communities in China. The term derives from the Arabic *qadîm* meaning 'old.' Their main characteristics were decentralization and isolation from each

other. They did trade among each other but kept their distances, especially from the Han communities due to a difference in culture and dietary laws. There was trade among the Muslim *gedimu*, which manifests itself in the frequent migrations that took place among the people. It was through the Sufi traditions and networks that they became more linked together than just in trading.

[227] Joseph Fletcher, "Sufi Paths (*taruq*) in China" an unpublished manuscript, Harvard University in Gladney, 41.

[228] Lipman, *Familiar Strangers*, 63.

[229] Joseph Fletcher, "The Naqsbandiyya in Northwest China" in *Studies on Chinese and Islamic Inner Asia*, Ed. Beatrice Manz (London: Variorum, 1995) 5-6.

[230] Ibid., 6.

[231] Ibid., 12.

[232] Ibid., 47.

[233] A debate over the *dhikr* would turn into one of the most controversial actions in China later on when another sub-branch of the Naqsbandiyya would be introduced that advocated a vocal *dhikr*. It would cause a lot of rebellion and bloodshed among the Muslim population itself. For further reference, see: Joseph Fletcher, "The Naqsbandiyya and the dhikr-i arra" in *Studies on Chinese and Islamic Inner Asia*, 175.

[234] Lipman, *Familiar Strangers*, 66.

[235] *Gongbei* were the tombs of the deceased Sufi leaders where adherents went to pray and were an important part of the daily ritual within the Sufi orders in China. For further reference on *gonbei* tombs, see: Jonathan Lipman, "Ethnic Violence in Modern China: Hans and Huis in Gansu, 1781-1929" in *Violence in China, Essays in Culture and Counterculture,* Jonathan N. Lipman, Steven Harrel, eds. (Albany: State University of New York Press, 1990) 70-71

[236] Ibid.

[237] Lipman," Ethnic Violence," 70-71.

[238] Fletcher, "The Naqsbandiyya," 21-22.

[239] For a copy of the text written by Wang, see: Lipman, *Familiar Strangers*, 76.

Notes to Chapter 6

[240] Israeli, 53.

[241] According to Nicole Grandin, the al-Mirghani family seems to show a long line of their family being important adherents to the Naqsbaniyya tariqa. For further reference on this subject, see: Nicole Grandin, "A propos des *Asânîd* de la Naqsbaniyya dans les fondements de la Khatmiyya du Soudan oriental: stratégies de pouvoir et relation maître/disciple," in *Les Rifâ'îs de Skopje Structure et Impact*, ed., Lijiljana Masulovic-Marsol, (Istanbul: Editions Isis).

[242] Voll, *Islam, Continuity and Change in the Modern World*, 147.

[243] Israeli, 156.

[244] Ma Mingxin had spent a considerable time in Yemen where he was introduced to the Sufi way and became associated with the order the Naqsbandiyya.

[245] It is important to point out Sufism was able to exist side by side with its Han counterpart despite its fundamentalist or purist message. This coexistence with non-Muslims was a trait that could be seen elsewhere with Sufi tariqas. For further treatment on Chinese coexistence, see: Jonathan N. Lipman, "Ethnic Violence," 69.

[246] Dillon, 23.

[247] Lipman, "Ethnic Violence," 75.

[248] For complete treatment on the subject, see: Fletcher, "The Naqsbandiyya and the dhikr -i- arra," 113, and Joseph Fletcher, "Les 'voies' (*taruq*) soufies en Chine" in *Les Ordres mystiques dan l'Islam*, Ed. A. Popovic, G. Veinstein (Paris: Editons de l'Ecole des Hautes Etudes en Sciences Sociale, 1986).

[249] The violence, which broke out, was under the guidance of the founders of the two sub-orders of the Naqsbandiyya, Ma Laichi and Ma Mingxin. It is pertinent that the Jahriyya was not a mainstream Naqsbandiyya order. *Jahriyya* suggests a vocal *dhikr* (loud prayer), which is usually associated with the Shiites and the following of Ali. The Naqsbandiyya is of Sunni origin, tracing its roots to Abu -Bakr who advocated a silent *dhikr*. The Naqsbandiyya is part of the Sunni tradition that usually follows a silent *dhikr*. For a full account, see: Israeli, Chapter 13.

[250] For a full account of the incident, see: Lipman, "Ethnic Violence," 69-71.

[251] For a full account on the rebellions occurring during the nineteenth century, see: Immanuel C. Y. Hsu, *The Rise of Modern China*, (New York: Oxford University Press, 1970) 270-311.

[252] The type of warfare usually waged by Muslims is known as *Jihad*, to conquer or convert those to the Islamic faith. This of course would not be the case in China. However, the Chinese Muslims could, if they banded together, cause serious disruption to the existing system.

[253] Lipman, "Ethnic Violence," 72.

[254] Israeli, 165.

[255] Part of Gansu has been detached to become the modern-day province of Ningxia.

[256] These rebellion are known in Western literature as the Panthay Rebellion., stemming from the Burmese word from Muslim. See: Hsu, 309.

[257] For full treatment on the subject, see: Richard Shek, "Sectarian Eschatology and Violence" in *Violence in China Essays in Culture and Counterculture*, Jonathan N. Lipman, Steven Harrell, eds. (Albany: State University of New York Press, 1990) 93-97.

[258] Israeli, 190.

[259] John Obert Voll, *Change and Continuity,"* 149.

[260] Hsu, 310.

[261] Colin Mackerras, *China's Minorities Integration and Modernization in the Twentieth Century* (Hong Kong: Oxford University Press, 1994) 41.

[262] Jinjibao is east of the Yellow River in the Gansu (Ningxia) region.

[263] Mackerras, 41.

[264] Gladney, 50.

[265] Dillon, 19.

[266] Lipman, "Ethnic Violence," 123, ff. 65.

[267] Israeli, 28.

[268] For a full treatment on Mahdism, see: Israel, 182-195.

[269] Lipman, "Ethnic Violence," 139.

[270] See: Israeli, 210.

[271] The Golden Age of Islam took place at the end of the seventh century and the beginning of the eighth century.

[272] Xinjiang today is constantly in a state of rebellion. Muslim terrorists have exploded bombs in Beijing, similar to the IRA in London.

Conclusion

[273] Cameroff, xv.

[274] C. E. Black, *The Dynamics of Modernization: A Comparative History* (New York: Harper and Row, 1967), 107-108.

Glossary

Arabic language

alim, sing. *ulema* pl. – religious scholar
amir – commander
baraka – beneficent force, of divine origin, which causes super-abundance in the physical sphere and prosperity and happiness in the physic order.
bayyt al-mal – house of wealth, meaning Treasury
darawish – dervishes
dhikr – drawn out repetition of the word Allah. It also means a basic repetition that is taught to those who follow Sufism.
fakie sing. *fugara*, pl. – a poor person, possibly even a beggar
fiqih – jurist
Fuqara – dervishes
Hadith – a statement or account of an action or saying of the Prophet Muhammed.
hakim – connotation of "judge"; in the Khatmiyya the title of an official who was entrusted with the duty of advising members on legal matters and who was authorized to intervene in disputes.
hijra – emigration of Muhammed from Mecca to Medina in 622 A. D. where he established the Muslim community-state
imam - leader; leader of a public prayer; spiritual and temporal leader in Shiite Islam.

Glossary

ijtihad – the action of using informed independent judgment in a legal or theological issue.

karama – performing miracles

khalifa- "successor" of Muhammed, caliph in Sunni Islam, deputy

khalifat al-khalifa - chief deputy; the head of the khalifas; a senior representative in an order

khanaqah - religious hostel; Sufi center.

al-khawass - the elect; the chosen

khawass al 0khawass - the elect of the elect

al-madrasa al-Idrisiyya- The Idrisiyya school

al-Mahdi - "the divinely guided; the person who will appear before the end of time to re-establish justice on earth

mu'allim - Quranic teacher

muqaddam - deputy; leader of a local branch in the Khatmiyya, assistant to the khalifa.

na'ib - deputy

qabila, sing. *qaba'ilun* pl.- tribe.

qadi - judicial official; judge who administers Sharia law.

qadi al-Islam - chief judge

al qadim - the ancient

shaukh - lit. "Old man"; also tribal chief; religious leader; head of a Sufi order.

silsila - chain of spiritual descent

siyasa - referring to governance, politics, administration

sunna - custom, saying or act of the Prophet.

taqlid - the unquestioning acceptance of the teachings of one of the Islamic schools of law.

tariqa sing. *Taruq or tariqas:* pl.- "path or way"; Sufi order or brotherhood.

tasawwuf - Sufi way or path

tawakkul - an absolute trust in God.

tajdid - the process of renewal

tariqa sing. *Taruq* pl. - "the way or the path", Sufi brotherhoods

tasawwuf – mysticism

tawakkul – an absolute trust in God
Zakat - Islamic tax; alms; charity.

Chinese language

gedimu – Chinese term for the Arabic *al-qadim*, meaning the ancient
gongbei – Sufi Saint's tomb.
Gubba – a saint's shrine
Hui hui – Chinese Muslims not belonging to a specific ethnic group
Hui jiao – Hui religion
Maitreya – a person who would usher in an era of peace and justice
menhuan – leading or saintly group; referring to *taruq*
minzu – from *shaoshu minzu*; there is no English translation of the word. The closest might be a group or sub-group

Bibliography

English language references

al-Afghani, Sayyid Jamal al-Din. "Islamic Solidarity" in *Islam in Transition*, eds. John L.
Donahue, John L. Esposito. New York: Oxford University Press, 1982.
Al-Shahi, Ahmad. "Sufism in Modern Sudan" in *Islam in the Modern World*, eds. Denis
  MacEoin, Ahmad Al-Shahi. New York: St. Martin's Press, 1983.
_____. "A Noah's Ark: the Continuity of the Khatmiyya Order in the northern Sudan",
  Bulletin, British Society for Middle Eastern Studies, viii 1, 1981.
Almond, Gabriel A., James S. Coleman. *The Politics of Developing Areas*. Princeton, N.J.: Princeton University Press, 1960.
  Anderson, Benedict. *Imagined Communities*, London: Verso, 1983.
An-Na'im, Abdullahi Ahmed. "Islam and Human Rights in Sahelian Africa" in *African Islam and Islam in Africa: Encounters between Sufis and Islamists*. eds. Eva Evers Rosander, David Westerlund. Athens, Ohio: Ohio University Press, 1977.
Al-Karsani, Awad Al-Sid, "Beyond Sufism: The Case of Millennial Islam in the Sudan" in *Muslim Identity and Social Change in Sub-Saharan Africa*. ed. Louis Brenner. Indianapolis: Indiana University Press, 1993.

Arberry, Arthur J. "Mysticism" in *The Cambridge History of Islam*. eds. Peter M. Holt,
Ann K. S. Lambton. Vol 2. Cambridge: Cambridge University Press, 1970.

Arendt, Hannah. "Communicative Power" in *Power*. ed. Stephen Lukes. Oxford: Blackwell, 1986.

Book XX of Al-Ghazali's Ihya' 'Ulum al-Din. (The Revitalization of the Sciences of Religion) Translated by L. Zolondek. Leiden: E. J. Brill, 1963.

Crecelius, Daniel. "The Course of Islam in Modern Egypt," in *Islam and Development: Religion and Sociopolitical Change*. ed. John L. Esposito. Syracuse: Syracuse University Press, 1980.

Camoroff, Jean and John Camoroff. *Modernity and Its Malcontents, Ritual and Power in Postcolonial Africa*. Chicago: Chicago University Press, 1993.

Coleman, James S. *International Encyclopedia of Social Sciences*, 1968 ed., vol. 10, s.v. "Modernization: Political Aspects," French and European Publishers.

Constantin, François. "Charisma and Power in East Africa" in *Charisma and Brotherhood in African Islam*, eds. Donal Cruise O'Brien, Christian Coulon. Oxford: Clarendon Press, 1988.

Cudsi, Alexander S. "Islam and Politics in the Sudan" in *Islam in the Political Process*. ed. James P. Piscatore. Cambridge: Cambridge University Press

Denny, Frederick Mathewson. *An Introduction to Islam*. New York: Macmillan Publishing Company, 1994.

Dillon, Michael. *China's Muslims*. Hong Kong: Oxford University Press, 1996.

Dore, R. P. "On the Possibility and Desirability of a Theory of Modernization". *Report: International Conference on the Problems of Modernization in Asia*, Asia Research Center, Korea University, Seoul, Korea.

Eickelman, Dale F., James Piscatore. *Muslim Politics*. Princeton: Princeton University Press, 1996.

Easton, David. "An Approach to the Analysis of Political Systems" in *World Politics* 9, no. 3. Princeton: Princeton University Press, 1957.

Elwell-Sutton, L. P. "Sufism and Pseudo-Sufism" in *Islam in the Modern World*. New York: St. Martin's Press, 1983.

Esposito, John L. *The Islamic Threat: Myth or Reality*. New York: Oxford University Press, 1992.

Fanon, Franz. "Violence Will be the Midwife of the New World" in *The Developing Nations What Path to Modernization?* ed. Frank Tachau. New York: Dodd, Mead & Co., 1974.

Farah, Caesar E. *Islam: Belief and Observances*, 5th Edition, New York: Barrons, 1990.

Fletcher, Joseph. "Sufi Paths (*taruq*) in China," an unpublished manuscript, Harvard University in Gladney, 41.

_____. "The Naqsbandiyya in Northwest China" in *Studies on Chinese and Islamic Inner Asia*. ed. Beatrice Manz. London: Variorum, 1995.

_____. "The Naqsbandiyya and the dhikr-i arra" in *Studies on Chinese and Islamic Inner Asia*.

Fleuhr-Lobban, Carolyn. "Islam in the Sudan: A Critical Study" in *Sudan, State and Society in Crisis*. ed. John O. Voll. Bloomington: Indiana University Press, 1991.

Friedrich, Carl J. *Man and His Government*. New York: 1963.

Gladney, Dru C. *Muslim Chinese Ethnic Nationalism in the People's Republic*. Harvard East Asian Monographs 149. Cambridge, Mass: Council on East Asian Studies, Harvard University, 1991.

Halpern, Manfred. "Political Parties" in *The Developing Nations What Path to Modernization?* ed. Frank Tachau. New York: Dodd, Meade & Co., 1974.

Hitti, Philip K. *A History of the Arabs,* 10th Edition. New York: St. Martin's Press, 1970.

Hobsbawn, Eric, Terence Ranger. *The Invention of Tradition*. Cambridge: Cambridge University Press, 1983.

Holt, P. M. *A Modern History of the Sudan*. New York: Grove Press, 1961.

_____. "The Islamization of the Nilotic Sudan" in *Northern Africa, Islam and Modernization*. ed. Michael Brett. London: Frank Cass, 1973.

_____. *The Mahdist State in the Sudan 1881-1898 a Study of Its Origins*

Development and Overthrow, 2nd Edition, Oxford: Clarendon, 1970.
Holt, P. M., M. W. Daly. *A History of the Sudan, From the Coming of Islam to the Present Day*. Boulder: Westview Press, 1979.
Hourani, Albert. *Arabic Thought in the Liberal age 1798-1939*. Cambridge: Cambridge University Press, 1983.
Huntington, Samuel P. "Political Modernization: America vs. Europe" in *World Politics*, vol. XVIII, April 3, 1966.
_____. "Political Development and Decay" in *Political Modernization*, ed. Claude E. Welch Jr. Belmont, CA: Wadsworth Publishing Co., 1967.
Immanuel, C. Y. Hsu. *The Rise of Modern China*, New York: Oxford University Press, 1970.
International Encyclopedia of Social Sciences. French and European Pubns., 1968 ed.
Israeli, Raphael. *Muslims in China, A Study in Cultural Confrontation*. London: Curzon Press, 1980.
Jenkins, R. G. "The Evolution of Religious Brotherhoods in North and Northwest Africa 1523-1900" in *Studies in West African Islamic History*.
Karrar, Ali Salih. *Sufi Brotherhoods in the Sudan*. Evanston, IL.: Northwestern University Press, 1992.
Kramer, Robert S. "Mahdi" in *The Encyclopedia of Modern Islam*, ed. John Esposito. New York: Oxford University Press, 1991.
Levtzion, Nehemiah and John O. Voll, *Eighteenth Century Renewal and Reform in Islam*. Syracuse: Syracuse University Press, 1987.
_____. "Eighteenth Century Sufi Brotherhoods, Structural, Organizational and Ritual Changes" in *Islam: Essays on Scripture, Thought and Society, A Festschrift in Honour of Anthony H. Johns*. eds. Peter G. Riddell, Tony Street. Leiden: Brill, 1997.
Lewis, Bernard. *The Political Language of Islam*. Chicago: The University of Chicago Press, 1988.
Lipman, Jonathan N. *Familiar Strangers A History of Muslims in Northwest China*. Seattle: University of Washington Press, 1997.
_____. "Ethnic Violence in Modern China: Hans and Huis in Gansu, 1781-1929" in *Violence in China, Essays in Culture and*

Counterculture. eds. Jonathan N. Lipman and Steven Harrel. Albany: State University of New York Press, 1990.

Mackerras, Colin. *China's Minorities Integration and Modernization in the Twentieth Century.* Hong Kong: Oxford University Press, 1994.

Mahmoud, Muhammed. "Sufism and Islamism in the Sudan" in *African Islam and Islam in Africa, Encounters between Sufis and Islamists.* eds. David Westerlund, Eva Evers Rosander. Athens, OH.: Ohio University Press, 1997.

Martin, B.G. *Muslim Brotherhoods in Nineteenth Century Africa.* Cambridge: Cambridge University Press, 1976.

Micaud, Charles. *Tunisia: The Politics of Modernization.* New York: Preager, 1964.

Najjar, Fauzi M. "*Siyasa* in Islamic Political Philosophy" in *Islamic Theology and Philosophy: Studies in Honor of George F. Hourani.* Albany: State University of New York Press, 1984.

Nasr, S. H. *Traditonal Islam in the Modern World.* London: 1987.

O'Brien, Donal B. Cruise. "Islam and Power in Black Africa" in *Islam and Power.* eds. Alexander C. Cudsi, Ali E. Dessouki. Baltimore, MD: John Hopkins University Press, 1981.

O'Brien, Donal B. Cruise and Christian Coulon, *Charisma and Brotherhood in African Islam.* Oxford: Clarendon Press, 1988.

O'Fahey, R. S. "Islamic Hegemonies in the Sudan" in *Muslim Identity and Social Change in Sub-Saharan Africa.* ed. Louis Brenner. Bloomington: Indiana University Press, 1993.

_____ and J. L. Spaulding, *Kingdoms of the Sudan.* London: 1974.

Olaniyan, Richard. "Islamic Penetration of Africa" in *African History and Culture.* ed. Richard Olaniyan. Lagos, Nigeria: Longman Nigeria Ltd., 1982.

Palmisano, Antonio. *Ethnicity: the Beja as Representation. Ethnizitat and Gesellschaft.* Occasional Paper 29. Berlin: Das Arabische Buch, 1991.

Pfaff, Richard F. "Disengagement From Traditionalism in Turkey and Iran" in *Western Political Quarterly.* vol. VI, March 1, 1963.

Lucien W. Pye, *Aspects of Political Development.* Boston: Little,

Brown & Company, 1966.
Qur'an, 49: 13, www.islamcity.com/Quran-Search.
Rahman, Fazlur. *Islam*. New York: Anchor Books, 1968.
_____. *Major Themes of the Qur'an*. Minneapolis, MN: Biblioteca Islamica, 1994.
Shek, Richard. "Sectarian Eschatology and Violence" in *Violence in China Essays in Culture and Counterculture*. eds. Jonathan N. Lipman, Steven Harrell. Albany: State University of New York Press, 1990.
Shepard, William. "What is Islamic Fundamentalism" in *Studies in Religion/Sciences Religieuses*. January 17, 1988.
Tibi, Bassam. *The Crisis of Modern Islam, A Preindustrial Culture in the Scientific-Industrial Age*. Salt Lake City, Utah: University of Utah Press, 1988.
Trimmingham, J. S. *Islam in the Sudan*. London: Oxford University Press, 1949.
_____. *The Sufi Orders in Islam*. Oxford: Clarendon Press, 1971.
Vergès, Merien. "Genesis of a Mobilization: The Young Activists of Algeria's Islamic Salvation Front" in *Political Islam Essays from Middle East Report*. eds. Joel Beinin and Joe Stork. Los Angeles, CA: University of California Press, 1997.
Vojas, E. "Problems Connected With Modernization of Underdeveloped Societies" in *Essays in Modernization of Underdeveloped Societies*. Bombay: Thacker and Co., 1971.
Voll, John O. "Sufi Thought and Practice" in *The Oxford Encyclopedia of the Modern Islamic World*. ed. John L. Esposito. New York: Oxford University Press, 1991.
_____. *Islam, Change and Continuity in the Modern World*. Syracuse: Syracuse University Press, 1994.
_____. "Mahdis, Walis, New Men in the Sudan" in *Scholars, Saints and Sufis, Muslim Religious Institutions Since 1500*. ed. Nikki R. Keddie. Berkeley: University of California Press, 1972.
_____. "A History of the Khatmiyya Tariqah in the Sudan", Ph.D. thesis, Harvard University,1969.
_____ and Sarah Potts. *The Sudan, Unity and Diversity in a Multicultural State*. Boulder: Westview Press, 1985.

Wallerstein, Immanuel, in *The Modern World System*. San Diego: Academic Press, 1980.

Warburg, Gabriel. *Historical Discord in the Nile Valley.* Evanston, IL.: Northwestern University Press, 1992.

_____. *Islam, Nationalism and Communism in a Traditional Society: the Case of the Sudan*. London: Frank Cass and Co., 1978.

Watt, W. Montgomery. *Muslim Intellectual: A Study of Al-Ghazali.* Edinburgh: The Edinburgh University Press, 1963.

Weber, Max. *Max Weber on Law in Economy and Society (Wirtshaft und Gesellschaft)*, 20th Century Legal Philosophy Series, ed. Max Rheinstein. Translated by Edward Shils and Max Rheinstein, vol. VI. Cambridge, MA: Harvard University Press, 1954.

_____. *Economy and Society*, eds. Guenther Roth, Claus Wittich. New York: Bedminister Press, 1968.

Wiarda, Howard J. "The Ethnocentrism of Social Science," in *Comparative Politics, Notes and Readings*.

Woodward, Peter. "Sudan: Islamic Radicals in Power" in *Political Islam Revolution, Radicalism or Reform?* ed. John L. Esposito. London: Lynne Rienner Publishers, 1997.

Foreign language references

Broudieu, Pierre. "La société traditionnelle," *Revue de sociologie du travail*. January-March, 1963.

Calvez, Jean-Yves. *Aspects Politique et Sociaux des Pays de Developpment*. Paris: Dalloz, 1971.

Delafosse, M. "L'Animisme nègre et sa resistance a l'Islamisation en Afrique occidentale," *R. M. M.*, Mars 1922, vol. XLIX.

Fletcher, Joseph. "Les 'voies' (*taruq*) soufies en Chine" in *Les Ordres mystiques dans l'Islam*. eds. A. Popovic, G. Veinstein. Paris: Editons de l'Ecole des Hautes Etudes en Sciences Sociale, 1986.

Grandin, Nicole. "Les taruq au Soudan dans la Corne de l'Afrique et en Afrique orientale" in *Les Ordres Mystiques Dans l'Islam Cheminements et situation actuelle*. eds. A. Popovic, G. Veinstein. Paris: Editions de l'Ecole des Hautes Etudes en Sciences Sociales, 1983.

_____. "A propos des *Asânîd* de la Naqsbaniyya dans les fondements de la Khatmiyya du Soudan oriental: stratégies de pouvoir et relation maître/disciple" in *Les Rifâ'îs de Skopje Structure et Impact*. ed. Lijiljana Masulovic-Marsol. Istanbul: Editions Isis.

Index

Abdallah, Muhammad Ahmad ibn, 52
Abu Dunana, Hammed, 35, 43
Ahmad, Muhammed, 20, 52, 56, 58-59, 62, 69, 74-77, 80-83, 107, 113-115
Ali, Muhammed, 47
Al-Afghani, 74-75
Al-Basri Hasan, 24
Al-Faruq, Khalifat, 59
Al-Gharbawi, Bishara, 34
Al-Ghazali, Abu Hamid, 25
Al-Hallaj, Husayn, 24
Al-Islam, 62
Al-Khawaww, Khawass, 45
Al-Khawass, 45
Al-Khulafa, Khalifat, 44
Al-Kunti, Al-Mukhtar, 37
Al-Mahdi, Sayyid 'Abd al-Rahman, 86
Al-Mirghani, Muhammed 'Uthman, 28, 40, 41
Al-Mirghani, Sayyid 'Ali, 88

Al-Qira'a, Shaykh, 43
Al-Rahman, Sayyid 'Abd, 88
Al-Saddiq, Khalifat, 59
Al-Sammani, Muhammed ibn Abd al-Karim, 39
Al-Shadhili, Husan, 35
Al-Tijani, Ahmad, 37
Al-Tayyib al-Bashir, Ahamd, 39
Al-Tahqiq, Shaykh, 43
Al-Tabarruk, Shaykh, 43
Al-Wahhab, Muhammad ibn Abd, 38; Wahhabi, 38
a minzu, 92
Almorvids (al-Murābitün), 6
Almoravid movement, 32
Ansar, 52-53, 57, 59, 61, 63, 86-89, 113
Arab, Idris ibn, 34
Ashigga, 88

Baraka, 34, 42-43, 56, 68-69, 76, 97; menhuan, 97
Baqqara tribes, 55, 60-61

Index 153

Bayt al-mal, 61

Chinese Muslims, 91
Christianity, 24-25
Colonialism, 84-87
Communist People's Republic, 109
Condominium Era, 87

Daiyu, Wang, 98
Danaqla, 60
Darfur, 33
Dark Ages, 11

Fanon, Franz, 82
Formation of the First politcal parties, 88; Socialist Republican Party; 88; National Unionist Party (NUP), 88; People's Democratic Party (PDP), 89
Funj sultanate, 6
Funj Kingdom, 33

Gansu, 95
Grandin, Nicole, 56; *gedimu*, 93
Great Rebellion, 101-102

Hadiths, 11
Hanafi School of, 93
Han Mandate of Heaven, 104
Hui hui, 91-92

Idris, Ahmad ibn, 40
Idrisiyya, 40

Ijtihad, 20
Islamic Fundamentalism, 10
Ismailis, 22

Ja'aliyyin, 60
Jilaniyya, 35

Khatmiyya, 20, 28
Khanaqahs, 27
Khartoum, 57
Kitab alAraba'in, 25

Maitreya, 103
Mahdist Revolution, 20
Mahdist state, 56
Mahdiyya, 51
Manchu, 103
Ma Hualong, 103
Ma Laichi, 95-97
Ma Mingxin, 99
Ming Dynasty, 92-93; Muslims in government, 94
Mirghaniyya, 28
Modernization theory, 11, 13
Muhammadiyya, Tariqa, 29
Mujdhubiyya, 54

Naqshbandiyya, 30, 95; Islamic identity, 95; Khufiyya, 97
Naqshband, Baha' ad-Din, 95
Na'ib, 44
Naqib, 44
National Unionist Party (NUP), 88
Neo-Mahdism, 86

Index

Neo-Sufism, 38
New Sect, 99
Nian Rebellion, 108
Ningxia region, 91

Omdurman, 57
Ottoman Empire, 84

People's Democratic Party (PDP), 89
Political party, 77-80
President Isma'il al-Azhari, 88

Qadiriyya, 35
Qinghai provinces, 91
Qing period, 94-95; Disharmony, 94

Revolutionary methods, 82
Revivalist movements, 99

Sacred authority, 68
Sammaniyya, 39
Shayqiyya, 41
Shadhiliyya, Shaykh Abu, 35
Sharia, 56
Sectarian, 105

Shoucair, Naum, 59
shura, 79
Silsila, 70
Sinnar, 33
Sinicization, 106
Siyasa, 25
Socialist Republican party, 88
Sufi origins, 23
Sunna, 11, 23
Sunni tradition, 93; China, 93

Tajdid, 10
Taiping Rebelion, 101
Tijaniyya, 29
Traditional authority, 70
Turko-Egyptian regime, 47-50
Twelvers, 22

Umma, 88

Wahhabi, 38
Wenxiu, Du, 104
White Lotus Society, 103

Zakat, 61
Zongtand, Zuo, 102

www.ingramcontent.com/pod-product-compliance
Lightning Source LLC
Chambersburg PA
CBHW022133080426
42734CB00006B/340